GOOD NEWS

The Kingdom ot GOD

TRAVIS DUNNIVAN

outskirts
press

Outskirts Press, Inc.
http://www.outskirtspress.com

ISBN: 978-1-9772-2461-3

PRINTED IN THE UNITED STATES OF AMERICA

Dedication

When I was younger I had a dog named Trigger. Trigger never cooked me a meal, and I don't think he ever remembered any of my birthdays. Trigger was not one to talk much, in fact he never spoke a word to me but I felt like I knew what he was saying when I looked into his eyes. When I was younger I probably did not ask why I loved that dog so much, but when I got older I thought about it and do you know what attracted me to that dog? I was attracted to Trigger because that dog loved me, that's exactly why I Love GOD.

1 John 4:19-21

> 19 We love because God first loved us. 20 If we say
> we love God, but hate others, we are liars. For we can-
> not love God, whom we have not seen, if we do not
> love others, whom we have seen. 21 The command that
> Christ has given us is this: whoever loves God must love
> others also.

I am pretty sure that GOD installed inside dogs the ability to love. So I am dedicating this book to Trigger and to GOD...thanks guys! Also in case you are wondering why we have been placed on this earth allow me to lay out the simple plan...#1 Love GOD, and #2 Love others.

Table of Contents

The Kingdom
Plain and Simple

Its a Kingdom of LOVE
Matthew 22:36-40

The book is about the Kingdom of GOD. When I started to try to piece together what JESUS was telling us in the parables, I discovered that the message that JESUS taught is not what I hear being taught in most churches. In fact it appears to me that large portions of the church are preaching a message contrary to what the scriptures teach. Some examples of what I am saying are found in Luke, John, and Acts

Luke 4:43

> But he said, "I must proclaim the good news of the <u>kingdom of God</u> to the other towns also, because that is why I was sent."

Unlike what many churches teach, JESUS did not mention the concept of eternity in heaven. Many churches would have you believe that JESUS came to earth so that each one of us could get a shot at going to heaven. Once we investigate the subject of heaven a little closer we find that heaven is not filled with saints that have passed.

John 3:13

> *No one has ever gone into heaven except the one who came from heaven-- (except) the Son of Man.*

In Acts 2 a concept is explained that many, many churches do not even mention. The earthly king David (whom GOD said the MESSIAH would descend from) lived a life and GOD said David was a man after the heart of GOD (Acts 13:22). After king David died, we are told that David is not currently sitting in heaven.

Acts 2:34-36

> *34 For <u>David did not ascend to heaven</u>, and yet he said,*
>
> *"'The LORD (GOD) said to my lord (king David):*
> *"Sit at MY right hand*
>
> *35 until I make your enemies*
> *a footstool for your feet."' or (until I put your enemies under your feet)*
>
> *36 "Therefore let all Israel be assured of this: <u>God has made this Jesus</u>, whom you crucified, <u>both LORD</u> and <u>MESSIAH</u>."*

From the way that I understand what the Bible is saying, is at the resurrection of the dead, king David is going to be resurrected and GOD is going to decree that king David be given some position of authority for 'eternity'. The scriptures do tell us that currently David is seated at the Right Hand of GOD. And David will remain seated at the Right Hand of GOD until GOD deals with the system that was opposed to king David. It is worth mentioning that believers are not living for themselves, so as a believer I do not have any enemies except the people that are part of the system that opposes GOD.

Of course the concept that heaven is not a location that people go to is not just some New Testament idea, even in the Old Testament it was understood that heaven is GOD's territory.

Psalms 115:16

> The heavens belong to the Lord, but the earth He has
> given to the children of men.

I feel that what the O.C. Supertones said describes why the 'church' is not my role model.

> 'Tell me who will listen to uneducated congregants
> And why should they when all we have to say is
> Bumper sticker doctrine and cute catch phrases
> Does this amaze us that no one will take us seriously'

Its easy to see that I am more than a little bit disappointed at the lack of intellectual honesty that has become 'church culture'. And I am fine with the fact that I do not operate exactly like the church. I feel that I try to view the world through different lenses.

One day, I walked into a store and observed a lady that was obviously having a bad day. I thought how the standard 'gospel' message might not be greatly accepted by the lady. The word gospel means 'good news', however I try to put myself in the shoes of other people and if they are not a christian then the only good news they will receive is that there is a way for them to die with confidence. I believe that the church has greatly misunderstood the message that is laid out in the Bible. Much of the church places a great deal of emphases on the death, burial, and resurrection of JESUS. While these events are very important, when JESUS was questioned by Pilate the death, burial, and resurrection was not mentioned.

John 18:37

> "You are a king, then!" said Pilate. Jesus answered, "You say that _I am a king_. In fact, _the reason_ I was born and came into the world _is to testify to the truth._ Everyone on the side of truth listens to me."

When Pilate found out that JESUS was "a king", JESUS said that the reason why HE was born was so that HE would be a martyr for the cause. There can be no martyrdom if everybody is on the same side, so by using deductive reasoning we can figure out that the reason why JESUS was born. JESUS was born to prove to the naysayers that HE was The KING! The death, burial, and resurrection of JESUS proved that the Kingdom of GOD is unlike any other kingdom because the top guy died for the bottom guy. The resurrection of CHRIST further proved that even the spirit of life and death are servants of the True KING!

The good news that the lady in the store needed to hear was 'your living life for an unjust master, but good news JESUS is The KING'. I explained to the lady that the kingdom of this world will soon pass away, but she could be apart of the Kingdom of GOD that will never pass away. Its fabulous news to find out that the point of earthly life is not able to be weighed or measured by human standards.

But I still think that the institutional church believes that 'the church system' is currently representational of the Kingdom of GOD, and I still think that they do not know what they are talking about. We know that the Kingdom of GOD is currently established in heaven. JESUS makes this idea plain when HE taught us to pray.

Matthew 6:10

> *Thy kingdom **come**, Thy will be done in earth, as it is in heaven.*

Because we know that the Kingdom of GOD is currently established in heaven. We can view heaven as the headquarters for the Kingdom that JESUS is KING of. This sheds a new light on 'why did GOD create earth'. Notice that GOD made the earth and everything and then for the grand finale GOD made mankind.

Genesis 1:28

> *And God blessed them [granting them certain authority] and said to them, "Be fruitful, multiply, and fill the earth, and subjugate it [putting it under your power]; and rule over (dominate) the fish of the sea, the birds of the air, and every living thing that moves upon the earth."*

But most people know the story about what happened after GOD granted authority to mankind. Mankind told GOD that they would just as soon build and manage there own kingdom. True followers of GOD have left there old life behind and are currently trying to manage affairs like the KING wants. For example it is not human nature (human nature is another way of saying 'the kingdom of mankind') to automatically respond to everybody in a Loving way.

The next story that I want to look at is the life of a man that told GOD that he wanted to do things his own way. The man was named king Nebuchadnezzar and he had a dream and the dream was interpreted by a servant of GOD.

Daniel 2:31-33

*31 "You, O king, were looking, and behold, [there was]
a single great statue; this image, which was large and of
unsurpassed splendor, stood before you, and its appear-
ance was awesome and terrifying. 32 As for this statue,
its head was made of fine gold, its breast and its arms of
silver, its belly and its thighs of bronze, 33 its legs of iron,
its feet partly of iron and partly of clay [pottery].*

The funny part of the dream comes in the next few verses. In the
dream the king also saw a stone smash the large statue, and then the
stone became a large mountain.

Daniel 2:34-35

*34 As you were looking, a stone (Matthew 21:42) was
cut out without [human] hands, and it struck the statue
on its feet of iron and clay and crushed them. 35 Then
the iron, the clay, the bronze, the silver, and the gold
were crushed together and became like the chaff from
the summer threshing floors; and the wind carried them
away so that not a trace of them could be found. And
the stone that struck the statue became a great mountain
(Hebrews 12:22-24) and filled the whole earth.*

The servant of GOD explains that the dream that GOD caused the
king to have, the statue represented earthly empires. The Kingdom of
GOD (which in the dream represented the stone that was not cut with
human hands) will smash all earthly kingdoms (as pictured on the
cover). As a side note, I want to point out that the Rock that smashes
the statue in Daniel 2 is the same Rock that JESUS said that HE was
going to build HIS 'church' on in Matthew 16:16-20.

16 Simon Peter replied, <u>"You (JESUS) are the Christ, the</u>
<u>*Son of the living God."*</u>

17 Jesus answered him, "Blessed are you, Simon son of
Jonah, for flesh and blood has not revealed this (confession) *to you, but My Father who is in heaven. 18 And I*
tell you that you are Peter (which means pebble that is
located along the path), *and on this rock* (the confession)
I will build My church, and the gates of Hades shall not
prevail against it. 19 I will give you the keys of the king-
dom of heaven, and whatever you bind on earth shall be
bound in heaven, and whatever you loose on earth shall
be loosed in heaven." 20 Then He commanded His disci-
ples to tell no one that He was Jesus the Christ (meaning
do not tell anyone that you are the king).

Of course the catholic church incorrectly assumes that what
JESUS said in the book of Matthew is Biblical proof that Peter (the
pebble) was appointed as the first pope (or head of the roman catholic church). But I think what the church is looking at is Biblical proof
that the papal succession (which Napoleon temporally halted...read
about Napoleon and the catholic church/pope pious vi) Or you can
read about the role that I see the catholic church playing

Revelation 13:12-13

12 He exercises all the authority of the first beast in his
presence and causes the earth and those who dwell on
it to worship the first beast, <u>whose deadly wound was</u>
<u>*healed*</u>. *13 He performs great signs, making fire come*
down from heaven on the earth in the sight of men.

Now moving on to the earthly life of JESUS CHRIST. When it was time for JESUS to begin HIS earthly ministry, the first words that came out of HIS mouth were about the Kingdom of GOD.

I want to comment on something that JESUS said, because it seems like a large portion of the church is ignoring HIS WORDs. In the following account JESUS whittled down a complex issue and made it easy for us to understand. It might seem like there are one million and one different gods to serve...but JESUS said that there were basicly two. Now the church has been saying that there are two opposing gods, but the way that the church makes things sound its a contest between GOD and satan.....hahahah! JESUS does not even give that washed up looser an honorable mention. JESUS tells us that the king and kingdom that opposes HIM is the desire for material gain (mammon).

Matthew 6:24

> *"No one can serve two masters. Either you will hate the one and love the other, or you will be devoted to the one and despise the other. You cannot serve both God (Choice #1) and mammon (Choice #2).*

I know a person that almost meets themselves coming and going to and from work. I know that the person is not happy, but I think that the thought is that they can 'defeat' mammon by accumulating a lot of worldly goods. But what the above person is doing is like trying to drink so much alcohol that it will wash away the fact that they are an alcoholic. I am going to share a secret 'every time you wrap one cord around the neck of mammon at the same time two cords are wrapped around your own neck.'

mammon is an unforgiving god... – *O.C. Supertones (Little Man)*

1 John 2:15-16

15 Do not love the world or the things in the world. If anyone loves the world, the love of the Father is not in him.16 For all that is in the world—the lust of the flesh, the lust of the eyes, and the pride of life—is not of the Father, but is of the world.

Salvation occurs when a person resolves to stop trying to build his or her own kingdom. Typically a person tries to build there own kingdom with mammon bricks. It is easy to think of mammon as just 'the love of money', but when a person engages in selfish behavior... that type of behavior belongs in the kingdom of mammon. The unjust master who is mammon will allow you to think that you are the master of your own domain (but get real and face the music...there is an invisible hand pushing you to do more and more work. You have met yesterday's goals but you are still unsatisfied.) That is because the master that you are serving is not fair. Mammon will allow you to think that you are accomplishing your goals, but its a lie.

If you are sick and tired of living your life and at the end of each day you end up with a handful of sand, thats because mammon is an unforgiving god. The cure for an empty life is to start serving LOVE, not only is GOD the KING but GOD is also LOVE and when a person chooses to model his or her life after LOVE then by default they are not working for the kingdom of mammon!

Fast forward through your life and hit the pause button when you get a chance to see your tomb stone. There will be two dates on the stone, one of the dates will be when you were born, the other date will be a record of when you died...but the dash mark that is between thoes two dates represents your life. If the LORD allows the tombstone to last for 100 years after you die, will that be your legacy? If you were able to write your highest achievement on the dash then in 100 years would it matter. The only thing on some peoples tombstones will be a record of there last words 'Here lies ____...he kept telling us that he was sick but nobody would believe him.'

I like to think about time travel, and sometimes I think about what person in history could shed light on various situations. If I was able to get into a time machine and go back 100 years and bring back to modern times the smartest doctor...I assume that the doctors knowledge and advice would be a bit out dated. The most astute lawyer from 100 years ago would be confused by some of today's laws. The person that had the greatest understanding of modern technology would sure impress me! However in the time machine example, when I go back 100 years and bring back a true Theologian, not only is the Theologians knowledge of the Bible still relevant today. But in many cases the old time Theologian could run circles around Bible scholars of today

I am not saying that it is wrong to be a mechanic, or a welder, I am just saying as you go through life keep your eyes on what is really going to have a lasting impact. In case you have failed to understand the way in which I write, I have tried to explain that the current doctrine of the 'church' would be able to offer little comfort to the lady that I met in the store. (Unless you would consider the fact that 'she is not going to be around for that much longer' to be 'good news')

But the real good news that I tried to share with the lady is that 'The Kingdom of GOD will soon lay waste to all the kingdoms of this world'. So life is normally a series of minor inconveniences, but if you continue to serve LOVE in spite of the temporary discomfort that it might cause you then you will be given a reward. Most people are drawn toward LOVE, but they soon give up and they try to enjoy the time that they are here on earth (I guess they suppose that they have been placed on earth so that they can take a vacation?) I am able to understand why some people have anxiety issues! The worlds screaming at them to run here and be like this...well I got good news... none of that junk matters. There was this guy named Charles Horton Kooley and one of the things that he pointed out was how confusing things can be when we assume that we know who we should be. It reminds me about the origins of 'Etiquette'. In 2400 B.C. An Egyptian guy by the name of Ptahhotep wrote a document that gave advice for Egyptian men climbing the social ladder of the day. One piece of advice was, "When sitting with one's superior, laugh when he laughs." Its like some peoples wedding reception...they spend huge amounts of money that they do not have, because they want to impress people that they do not know.

Make sure to brush up on your etiquette, because without it you might not be able to impress all the right people that really do not matter. I want people to like me, and I think that a person should be polite and courteous to others, but the truth of the matter is that its to bad (for you) if you think that my shoes do not match with my shirt. In my mind many anxiety issues exists because the person is having an identity crisis. So in support of your mental health, read what GOD has to say about humanity in the Bible! Remember how unforgiving mammon is, do not think that mammon will go easy on you for the sake of your mental health.

It seems to me that some people's (and not all cases) of anxiety are simply a misunderstanding of 'who really matters'. Much of the church wants to paint a picture like JESUS is best depicted on a stain glass window, but let me make very clear the fact that GOD is LOVE...I did not say that GOD is like LOVE or GOD has a lot of LOVE...GOD is the personification of LOVE!

1 John 4:8-11

8 Anyone who does not love does not know God, for God is love. 9 In this way the love of God was revealed to us, that God sent His only begotten Son into the world, that we might live through Him. 10 In this is love: not that we loved God, but that He loved us and sent His Son to be the atoning sacrifice for our sins. 11 Beloved, if God so loved us, we must also love one another.

I am going to speak to the church leaders that are hiding behind their lists of man made doctrines. I understand that you feel the need to cast stones when people violate the sacred rules, now I want you to understand that unless someones lifestyle is in direct opposition with what the Bible says, then you are throwing stones at people because they broke the rules of 'your kingdom'. Not only has GOD vowed to smash other kingdoms along with those who build them, but GOD is jealous for a holy bride (like a mother bear is jealous for her cubs). I am uncertain what name that you want me to use, but I think that the name stupid can be used to describe someone that is arrogantly pestering something that GOD LOVES

Revelation 19:11-21

11 I saw heaven opened. And there was a white horse. He who sat on it is called Faithful and True, and in righteousness He judges and wages war. 12 His eyes are like a flame of fire, and on His head are many crowns. He has a name written, that no one knows but He Himself. 13 He is clothed with a robe dipped in blood. His name is called The Word of God. 14 The armies in heaven, clothed in fine linen, white and clean, followed Him on white horses. 15 Out of His mouth proceeds a sharp sword, with which He may strike the nations. "He shall rule them with an iron scepter." He treads the wine press of the fury and wrath of God the Almighty. 16 On His robe and on His thigh He has a name written:

KING OF KINGS
AND LORD OF LORDS.

(JESUS is the KING that is over all the people that consider themselves to be kings, and anyone that thinks that they are a high ranking lord is a servant to the LORD!)

17 And I saw an angel standing in the sun, and he cried with a loud voice to all the birds flying in the midst of heaven, "Come and gather for the supper of the great God, 18 to eat the flesh of kings, the flesh of commanders, the flesh of strong men, the flesh of horses and their riders, and the flesh of all men, both free and slave, both small and great!"

19 Then I saw the beast and the kings of the earth with their armies gathered to wage war against Him who sat on the horse and against His army. 20 But the beast was captured and with him the false prophet who worked signs in his presence, by which he deceived those who received the mark of the beast and those who worshiped his image. These two were thrown alive into the lake of fire that burns with brimstone. 21 The remnant were slain with the sword which proceeded out of the mouth of Him who sat on the horse. And all the birds gorged themselves with their flesh.

In short, the Kingdom of GOD dominates. So what is the responsibility of us Kingdomites? Well the more literal that are among us might think that people are to open 'zoos and aquariums'. While you can do that, what is actually meant by Genesis 1:28 is that we are responsible for making sure that we are light bearers. A torch can not be placed into a dark room without the darkness being disturbed. So if you want to be a light bearer at the zoo that you open...then do that! But if you feel that the most strategic location for you to be a light bearer is in a auto mechanic shop then you should do that!

The Kingdom of GOD is not totally in the realm that humans exist in. Although a Kingdomite might be walking around in the human realm that person is laboring to recruit others to deny there own desires and follow CHRIST.

Maby you are thinking that you are prohibited from sharing your faith in certain situations. Well you have been listening to the 'church' for two long, the conversations of the church resembles a one string fiddle. But The Kingdom of GOD is not set up to be anything like the structure of the church. Both say that they want the world to be shaped into the image of CHRIST, but that is when the church starts to string up there fiddle. The Kingdom of GOD does want people to come to a saving knowledge of JESUS CHRIST, but situations need to be approached in a more intelligent manner. In Matthew The KING gave us instructions on how to evangelize the world.

Matthew 10:16-17

> 16 Look, I am sending you out as sheep in the midst of wolves. Therefore be wise as serpents and harmless as doves. 17 But beware of men, for they will deliver you up to the councils, and they will scourge you in their synagogues.

Many church members act like they were told to be as dumb as sheep and vicious like wolves. Many people (both Christians and non Christians alike) do not understand that GOD put up certain boundaries to protect people. Crossing those boundaries is 'sin'. In and of itself, sin is bad...but it sin, or living life on your own terms, is also damaging. The church system assumes that the only reason why anyone should want to stop living life on there own terms is for reasons that will not be seen until the future, but I am telling you that people should stop sinning because 'sin messes things up'! Look at the world and consider who is shaping it. If you think that the whole operation runs more smoothly when everybody does what they want, then you are certainly misguided!

Suppose I created a product, and on the package I put a warning label 'do not get product wet'. After buying the product you decide that you should take the product to the pool. I did not include a warning label so that I could control things. Not only did you 'sin' or miss the mark, but now you have a damaged product. It relay does not matter how good of an excuse you had of why you took it to the pool. The fact remains that the product was not designed to get wet. When GOD created us HE was nice enough to include a 'users manual', and to make sure that the users manual was understood GOD designed THE BEST SALESMAN to give a product demonstration.

Let me give a real life application. I am against killing innocent babies for the sake of convenience. The KING teaches to value life, and I am not going to go against the KING! Some people might throw all kinds of insults at me, but if I just ask myself 'Why would the KING tell a society that they are to value human life?' then the answer becomes more clear to me. Every earthly economy is dependent on trade. Trading requires one buyer and one seller. The population of the United States is around 327 million people (or 327 million potential traders). Since 1973 there have been an estimated 50 million abortions in the United States. Basicly what has been done is this society has reduced the number of traders that it has by roughly 15%. Just looking at what has been done from a logistical stand point, the word 'stupid' describes what has been done. So if you are a person that supports abortion and if you have ever been disappointed because someone does not have a job or you do not make enough money, have you yet to realize that maby the baby that you supported the murder of, maby in an alternate time line that baby was going to give the unemployed a job. Maby the baby would have grown up to create a business that would have increased the value of your job... yep people that do not follow the KING they are some real looser!

Maby you would say 'Travis that example is too gloomy to speak of'. Then let us discuss another arena that the ignorance of the church has left unprotected. If evolution is such a rock solid theory, then how many giraffe heads exploded before a system of valves 'evolved out of necessity'. I am no where near the height of a giraffe, and when I hang upside down for to long it feels like my head might explode. Maby the first giraffe knew that it should not bend over and eat grass on account of all the blood that was in its neck. In fact that first giraffe remembered that it should not bend over for maby a million years The giraffes that we know today obviously forgot the animalistic instincts of the early giraffes because today giraffes bend over. Of course if the long neck of the giraffe evolved to reach a higher food source, then why does its neck bend at all. Another concept that the church does not think about is that a pair of male and female giraffes must have been going through the same evolutionary changes, because if there was not two different sets of chromosomes then how would reproduction occur? So by looking at just the giraffe the theory of evolution is about as likely as constantly being struck by a bolt of lightning as a person traveled from California to New York.

Rather than me attempting to speak about subjects that I know little about, let me just try to point to an explanation of how a Kingdomite should live. However I will point out that the church system has done a very poor job at teaching people that serving the KING does not mean that a person will no longer need a brain, the opposite is true if a person uses there brain they will realize that some force/being designed things to operate a certain way and if they try to violate the 'terms of use' then a malfunction will occur!

Proverbs Introduction

I have tried to explain how the 'church' has hijacked the message of the Kingdom of GOD. In doing so, I have pointed out how the church has ignored what GOD has said, so if what I have done is compared to attempting to erasing some of what the church has taught... then I am o.k. with that. However JESUS taught that once incorrect things are removed a void is created, and that void will become filled once again (Matthew 12:43-46). I did not write this book so that people would abandon the profane teachings that they have been taught by the church system, just so a more grotesque teaching would be able to fill the empty void. So in the next few pages, I am going to be sharing some of the principals that the Bible says should be in peoples lives. While this book is intended to cause individuals to question and in some cases move away from what they have been taught by the church system, the book is also intended to help point to information that the Bible says should be present in the lives of believers.

Just like a farmer spends time learning about seeds, also should people that align themselves with the Kingdom of GOD spend time learning about how they should behave. In the Kingdom of GOD the way that 'Kingdomites' should behave is known as Wisdom.

Now what nuggets of wisdom do I posses that can radially transform people's lives? Well, I am not trying to stand on my own! Fortunately the KING is much, much, much smarter than me, and HE has already written Wisdom principals. Of course the Bible contains more Wisdom principals than what I am including in this book and as we will find out becoming more and more Wise is a lifelong pursuit.

In the coming pages I am going to try to teach from a very important book of the Bible. One of the most beloved passages in Proverbs speaks about what GOD did first, and the first thing that GOD created was 'lady Wisdom'. Think about that! GOD created a lot of things but the one thing that GOD determined should be created first was Wisdom (Proverbs 8:22-31). Creation is much more complicated than building a building or paving a road, but from those petty examples we can understand the importance of a strong foundation. Now put the two thoughts together, GOD named the foundation of all life, Wisdom. What many people have more than likely not been taught is that Wisdom is definitely not just another 'gadget' in a persons utility belt. Instead walking around without Wisdom is like walking around without legs.

It is important to remember that Proverbs is not written to be used as an exact users manual. Instead think of Proverbs as a respectable tour guide that is teaching people how to develop a more sophisticated style. Imagine that when you first entered the art gallery, all of the paintings looked like blobs of paint. But after being coached by the tour guide you were able to see the outline of certain images. And the more time that you spent looking at the paintings then the more images that came into focus. A person can read the book of Proverbs repeatedly for years and then one day information just 'clicks', and the WORD's come into greater focus!

The book of Proverbs is a book of Hebrew poetry, so after the translation of the foreign language has been made there are still some cultural differences. Kind of like a foreigner might speak your native language, but sometimes ideas get lost in translation. With that being said the main theme of Proverbs is 'If a person does not greatly reverence GOD, then they can not begin to understand Wisdom'. (Proverbs 1:7)

The first 9 chapters of the book is written like the advice that you would hear a teacher giving. Proverbs chapter 10 through chapter 29 is usually written in two-line poetic couplets.

(ex.) *Proverb 10:4*

> *Lazy hands make for poverty,*
> *but diligent hands bring wealth.*

Proverbs chapter 30 and the beginning of chapter 31, are two more sections of advice. And Proverbs 31:10-31 is an acrostic (an acrostic poem is a poem in which the initial letters of each successive line form a word, phrase or pattern). But some of the 'poeticness' of the book is lost when the original language was translated from Hebrew.

It's true that I am trying to drill Wisdom literature into people because...well thats the model that GOD showed me **Proverbs 8:22**. But aside from that preachers have done an extreme disservice by teaching people that the enemy of every person has a pitchfork and horns. I want people to realize that the enemy that they face is themselves. Its true that **James 1:13** identifies that each of us is our own personal devil, but I want people to see things abit more clearly.

In the passage below, Paul is describing an internal battle that is a conflict that each of us needs to deal with.

Romans 7:22-23

> *22 For deep down I am in happy agreement with God's law* (the law of the KING); *23 but the rest of me does*

not concur. I see a very different principle at work in my bodily members, and it is at war with my mind; I have become a prisoner in this war to the rule of sin in my body (the law of mammon).

Paul was saying that he was more than happy to live by The KING's rules, but there was a conflict raging inside of himself and it is a struggle for him to do the things that are right. The reason why I am mentioning that teaching during the introduction to Proverbs is this: sin has a way of transforming people (The term 'sin' comes from the world of archery and it means 'to miss the mark'. The mark is for us to live by The KING's rules.) When a person sin's, they have opened the floodgate and invited many problems into their lives. Living a wise lifestyle will help to prevent a lot of grief!

The Book of Proverbs

Chapter 1:

The Purpose and Theme

1 The proverbs of Solomon, the son of David, king of Israel:

2 To know wisdom and instruction,
   to perceive the words of understanding,

3 to receive the instruction of wisdom,
   justice, judgment, and equity;

4 to give subtlety {skill in achieving one's ends through indirect
   means} to the simple,
   to the young man knowledge and discretion—

5 a wise man will hear and will increase learning,
   and a man of understanding will attain wise counsel,

6 to understand a proverb and the interpretation,
   the words of the wise and their riddles.

7 The fear of the Lord is the beginning of knowledge,
   but fools despise wisdom and instruction.

8 My son, hear the instruction of your father (as a teacher to his stu-
   dent),
   and do not forsake the teaching of your mother;

9 for they will be a garland of grace on your head,
   and chains about your neck.

10 My son, if sinners entice you,
   do not consent. (A warning against bad company)

   {1 Corinthians 15:3 Do not be deceived: "Bad company corrupts good character."}

11 If they say, "Come with us,
   let us lie in wait for blood;
   let us lurk secretly for the innocent without cause;

12 let us swallow them up alive as the grave,
   and whole, as those who go down into the pit;

13 we will find all kinds of precious possessions;
   we will fill our houses with spoil;

14 cast in your lot among us,
   let us all have one purse—

15 my son, do not walk in the way with them,
   keep your foot from their path;

16 for their feet run to evil
   and make haste to shed blood.

17 Surely in vain the net is spread
   in the sight of any bird.

18 They lie in wait for their own blood;
   they lurk secretly for their own lives.

19 So are the ways of everyone who is greedy of gain,
   which takes away the life of its owners.

The Call of Wisdom

20 Wisdom cries out in the street;
   she utters her voice in the markets.

21 She cries at the corner of the streets, in the openings of the gates;
   she speaks her words in the city, saying:

22 "How long, you simple ones, will you love simplicity?
   For the scorners delight in their scorning,
   and fools hate knowledge.

23 Turn at my reproof;
   surely I will pour out my spirit on you;
   I will make my words known to you.

24 Because I have called and you refused,
   I have stretched out my hand and no man regarded,

25 because you neglected all my counsel,
   and would have none of my reproof,

26 I also will laugh at your calamity;
   I will mock when your fear comes,

27 when your fear comes as desolation
   and your destruction comes as a whirlwind,
   when distress and anguish come upon you.

28 "Then they will call on me, but I will not answer;
   they will seek me early, but they will not find me.

29 Because they hated knowledge
   and did not choose the fear of the Lord,

30 they would have none of my counsel
   and despised all my reproof.

31 Therefore they will eat of the fruit of their own way,
   and be filled with their own devices.

32 For the turning away of the simple will slay them,
   and the prosperity of fools will destroy them.

33 But whoever listens to me will dwell safely,
   and will be secure from fear of evil."

Note: Proverbs 1:20 Lady Wisdom is personified, and is referred to as a female.

Chapter 2:

The Value of Wisdom

1 My son, if you will receive my words,
   and hide my commandments within you,

2 so that you incline your ear to wisdom,
   and apply your heart to understanding;

3 yes, if you cry out for knowledge,
   and lift up your voice for understanding,

4 if you seek her as silver,
   and search for her as for hidden treasures,

5 then you will understand the fear of the Lord,
   and find the knowledge of God.

6 For the Lord gives wisdom;
   out of His mouth come knowledge and understanding.

7 He lays up sound wisdom for the righteous;
   He is a shield to those who walk uprightly.

8 He keeps the paths of justice,
   and preserves the way of His saints.

9 Then you will understand righteousness and judgment
   and equity, and every good path.

10 When wisdom enters your heart,
   and knowledge is pleasant to your soul,

11 discretion will preserve you;
   understanding will keep you,

12 to deliver you from the way of the evil man,
   from the man who speaks perverse things,

13 from those who leave the paths of uprightness
   to walk in the ways of darkness;

14 who rejoice to do evil,
   and delight in the perversity of the wicked;

15 whose ways are crooked,
   and who are devious in their paths;

16 to deliver you from the immoral woman,
   even from the seductress who flatters with her words,

17 who forsakes the guide of her youth,
   and forgets the covenant of her God.

18 For her house leads down to death,
   and her paths to the departed spirits;

19 none who go to her return again,
   nor do they take hold of the paths of life.

20 So you may walk in the way of good men
  and keep the paths of the righteous.

21 For the upright will dwell in the land,
  and the innocent will remain in it;

22 but the wicked will be cut off from the earth,
  and the transgressors will be rooted out of it.

Note: v. 12 (part-a) "to deliver you from the way of the evil man" The phrase "from the way" is the Hebrew word mid·de·reⱬ and the word refers to a -course of life or mode of action-. This verse is not telling us that Wisdom will protect us from being associated with the punishment of people that are in the wrong crowd, but Wisdom will place us on a different course in life (In fact Proverbs 13:17 teaches people that fools breed foolishness). The more wise that a person becomes then the more 'odd' that you will appear to foolish people because a foolish person can not see what you are trying to avoid.

Chapter 3:

The Rewards of Wisdom

1 My son, do not forget my teaching,
  but let your heart keep my commandments;

2 for length of days and long life
  and peace will they add to you.

3 Do not let mercy and truth forsake you;
  bind them around your neck,
  write them on the tablet of your heart,

4 so you will find favor and good understanding
   in the sight of God and man.

5 Trust in the Lord with all your heart,
   and lean not on your own understanding;

6 in all your ways acknowledge Him,
   and He will direct your paths.

7 Do not be wise in your own eyes;
   fear the Lord and depart from evil.

8 It will be health to your body,
   and strength to your bones.

9 Honor the Lord with your substance,
   and with the first fruits of all your increase;

10 so your barns will be filled with plenty,
    and your presses will burst out with new wine.

11 My son, do not despise the chastening of the Lord,
    nor be weary of His correction;

12 for whom the Lord loves He corrects,
    even as a father the son in whom he delights.

13 Happy is the man who finds wisdom,
    and the man who gets understanding;

14 for her benefit is more profitable than silver,
    and her gain than *fine* gold.

15 She is more precious than rubies,
    and all the things you may desire are not to be compared with
    her.

16 Length of days is in her right hand,
   and in her left hand riches and honor.

17 Her ways are ways of pleasantness,
   and all her paths are peace.

18 She is a tree of life to those who take hold of her,
   and happy is everyone who retains her.

19 The Lord by wisdom has founded the earth;
   by understanding He has established the heavens;

20 by His knowledge the depths are broken up,
   and the clouds drop down the dew.

21 My son, let them not depart from your eyes—
   keep sound wisdom and discretion;

22 so they will be life to your soul
   and grace to your neck.

23 Then you will walk safely in your way,
   and your foot will not stumble.

24 When you lie down, you will not be afraid;
   yes, you will lie down and your sleep will be sweet.

25 Do not be afraid of sudden terror,
   nor of trouble from the wicked when it comes;

26 for the Lord will be your confidence,
   and will keep your foot from being caught.

27 Do not withhold good from those to whom it is due,
   when it is in the power of your hand to do it.

28 Do not say to your neighbor,

"Go, and come again, and tomorrow I will give it,"
when you have it with you.

29 Do not devise evil against your neighbor,
seeing he dwells securely by you.

30 Do not strive with a man without cause,
if he has done you no harm.

31 Do not envy the oppressor,
and choose none of his ways;

32 for the perverse is an abomination to the Lord,
but His secret *counsel* is with the righteous.

33 The curse of the Lord is on the house of the wicked,
but He blesses the habitation of the just.

34 Surely He scorns the scornful,
but He gives favor to the humble.

35 The wise will inherit glory,
but shame will be the legacy of fools.

<v. 5-6 Reminds us that humans have a limited amount of knowledge. If all the information that humans understand was represented by water, then we could not even fill up an eye dropper. However, if a small portion of what GOD understands was represented by water then that amount of knowledge would be more vast than all of the oceans. Not every decision (that you should make) is going to make the most sense to you, but just because you do not understand why GOD said something that is in the Bible that does not make it wrong. So place your trust in what GOD says even if what is said goes against conventional thought.

<v. 35 Gives a clear definition of the two different paths. Have you thought about what kind of legacy that you are laying down behind you? Its like the saying 'if you aim at nothing then you will probably hit it.'

Chapter 4:

Wisdom Is Supreme

1 Hear, O children, the instruction of a father,
   and attend to know understanding.

2 For I give you good precepts;
   do not forsake my teaching.

3 For I was my father's son,
   tender and the only beloved in the sight of my mother.

4 He also taught me and said to me,
   "Let your heart retain my words;
   keep my commandments, and live.

5 Get wisdom! Get understanding!
   Do not forget it, nor turn away from the words of my mouth.

6 Do not forsake her, and she will preserve you;
   love her, and she will keep you.

7 Wisdom is principal; therefore get wisdom.
   And with all your getting, get understanding.

8 Exalt her, and she will promote you;
   she will bring you honor, when you embrace her.

9 She will place on your head an ornament of grace;
   a crown of glory she will deliver to you."

10 Hear, my son, and receive my sayings,
   and the years of your life will be many.

11 I have taught you in the way of wisdom;
   I have led you in right paths.

12 When you walk, your steps will not be hindered,
   and when you run, you will not stumble.

13 Take firm hold of instruction, do not let her go;
   keep her, for she is your life.

14 Do not enter the path of the wicked,
   and do not go in the way of evil men.
   15 Avoid it, do not travel on it;
   turn from it and pass on.

16 For they do not sleep unless they have done mischief;
   and their sleep is taken away unless they cause some to fall.

17 For they eat the bread of wickedness
   and drink the wine of violence.

18 But the path of the just is as the shining light,
   that shines more and more unto the perfect day.

19 The way of the wicked is as darkness;
   they do not know at what they stumble.

20 My son, attend to my words;
   incline your ear to my sayings.

21 Do not let them depart from your eyes;
   keep them in the midst of your heart;

22 for they are life to those who find them,
   and health to all their body.

23 Keep your heart with all diligence,
   for out of it are the issues of life.

24 Put away from you a deceitful mouth,
   and put perverse lips far from you.

25 Let your eyes look right on,
   and let your eyelids look straight before you.

26 Ponder the path of your feet,
   and let all your ways be established.

27 Do not turn to the right or to the left;
   remove your foot from evil.

v.26 Sometimes people stumble just because they do not think about what 'reaction' will take place, but remember that every action will produce a reaction.

Chapter 5:

Warning Against Adultery

1 My son, attend to my wisdom,
   and bow your ear to my understanding,

2 that you may regard discretion,
   and that your lips may keep knowledge.

3 For the lips of an immoral woman drip as a honeycomb,
   and her mouth is smoother than oil.

4 But her end is bitter as wormwood,
   sharp as a two-edged sword.

5 Her feet go down to death,
   her steps take hold of Sheol.

6 She does not ponder the path of life;
   her ways are unstable, and she does not know it.

7 Hear me now therefore, O children,
   and do not depart from the words of my mouth.

8 Remove your way far from her,
   and do not go near the door of her house,

9 lest you give your honor to others,
   and your years to the cruel;

10 lest strangers be filled with your wealth,
   and your labors go to the house of a stranger;

11 and you mourn at the last,
   when your flesh and your body are consumed,

12 and say, "How I have hated instruction,
   and my heart despised reproof!

13 And I have not obeyed the voice of my teachers,
   nor inclined my ear to those who instructed me!

14 I was almost in utter ruin
   in the midst of the congregation and assembly."

15 Drink waters out of your own cistern,
   and running waters out of your own well.

16 Should your fountains be dispersed abroad,
   streams of water in the streets?

17 Let them be only your own,
   and not for strangers with you.

18 Let your fountain be blessed,
   and rejoice with the wife of your youth.

19 Let her be as the loving deer and pleasant doe;
   let her breasts satisfy you at all times;
   and always be enraptured with her love.

20 Why should you, my son, be intoxicated by an immoral woman,
   and embrace the bosom of a seductress?

21 For the ways of man are before the eyes of the Lord,
   and He ponders all his goings.

22 His own iniquities entrap the wicked himself,
   and he is snared in the cords of his sins.

23 He will die for lack of instruction,
   and in the greatness of his folly he will go astray.

< v.3 The passage is not just speaking of fast women, the Hebrew word that is used is zuwr (zoor) and it is the same phrase that is used in Leviticus 10:1 to describe what two men offered to the LORD. Leviticus 10:1 *Now Nadab and Abihu, the sons of Aaron, took their respective firepans, and after putting fire in them, placed incense on it and offered strange fire before the LORD, which He had not commanded them.* I think the lesson that is being taught is that ..."*Bad company corrupts good character.*" (1 Corinthians 15:33) So choose your friends wisely because all that glitters is not gold.>

Chapter 6:

Warning Against Pledges

1 My son, if you put up a security for your friend,
   if you have shaken hands with a stranger,

2 you are snared with the words of your mouth;
   you are taken with the words of your mouth.

3 Do this now, my son, and deliver yourself;
   when you have come into the hand of your friend,
   go and humble yourself;
   plead with your friend.

4 Give no sleep to your eyes,
   nor slumber to your eyelids.

5 Deliver yourself as a doe from the hand of the hunter,
   and as a bird from the hand of the fowler.

The Folly of Idleness

6 Go to the ant, you sluggard!
   Consider her ways and be wise.

7 Which, having no guide,
   overseer, or ruler,

8 provides her bread in the summer,
   and gathers her food in the harvest.

9 How long will you sleep, O sluggard?
   When will you arise out of your sleep?

10 Yet a little sleep, a little slumber,

a little folding of the hands to sleep—

11 so will your poverty come upon you like a stalker,
and your need as an armed man.

The Wicked Man

12 A wayward person, a wicked man,
walks with a perverse mouth.

13 He winks with his eyes,
he signals with his feet,
he motions with his fingers;

14 perversity is in his heart,
he devises mischief continually, he sows discord.

15 Therefore his calamity will come suddenly;
in a moment he will be broken without remedy.

16 These six things the Lord hates,
yes, seven are an abomination to him:

17 a proud look,
a lying tongue,
and hands that shed innocent blood,

18 a heart that devises wicked imaginations,
feet that are swift in running to mischief,

19 a false witness who speaks lies,
and he who sows discord among brethren.

Warning Against Adultery

20 My son, keep your father's commandment,
   and do not forsake the instruction of your mother.

21 Bind them continually upon your heart,
   and tie them around your neck.

22 When you go, they will lead you;
   when you sleep, they will keep you;
   and when you awake, they will speak with you.

23 For the commandment is a lamp, and the law is light;
   and reproofs of instruction are the way of life,

24 to keep you from the evil woman,
   from the flattery of the tongue of a seductress.

25 Do not lust after her beauty in your heart,
   nor let her allure you with her eyelids.

26 For by means of a harlot a man is reduced to a piece of bread,
   and the adulteress will prey upon his precious life.

27 Can a man take fire in his bosom,
   and his clothes not be burned?

28 Can one walk upon hot coals,
   and his feet not be burned?

29 So he who goes in to his neighbor's wife;
   whoever touches her will not be innocent.

30 Men do not despise a thief if he steals
   to satisfy himself when he is hungry.

31 But if he is found, he will restore sevenfold;
   he will give all the substance of his house.

32 But whoever commits adultery with a woman lacks understanding;
he who does it destroys his own soul.

33 A wound and dishonor will he get,
and his reproach will not be wiped away.

34 For jealousy is the rage of a man;
therefore he will not spare in the day of vengeance.

35 He will not regard any ransom,
nor will he rest content, though you give many gifts.

v.1-2 'Be careful about the company that you keep'. The word
that is translated is also used to describe an opponent. Not only do
you need to consider your way but its a good idea to consider the
ways of the people around you.

v.6-8 A message of how foolish it is to just float through life and
expect to not run into trouble. If you aim at nothing, then you will
probably waste a lot of time and energy trying to accomplish the goal.
We are told to act like the ants, they do not just rejoice during the
times of plenty. Instead the ant uses the time of plenty to prepare for
meager times.

Chapter 7:

Beware of the Adulteress

1 My son, keep my words,
and lay up my commandments within you.

2 Keep my commandments and live,
and my teaching as the apple of your eye.

3 Bind them on your fingers;
   write them on the tablet of your heart.

4 Say to wisdom, "You are my sister,"
   and call understanding your kinswoman,

5 that they may keep you from the immoral woman,
   from the seductress who flatters with her words.

6 For at the window of my house
   I looked through my casement,

7 and saw among the simple ones,
   I discerned among the youths,
   a young man void of understanding,

8 passing through the street near her corner;
   and he went the way to her house

9 in the twilight, in the evening,
   in the black and dark night.

10 And there a woman met him,
    with the attire of a harlot, and subtle of heart.

11 She is loud and stubborn;
    her feet do not abide in her house.

12 Now she is without, now in the streets,
    and lies in wait at every corner.

13 So she caught him, and kissed him;
    and with an impudent face said to him:

14 "I have peace offerings with me;
    this day have I paid my vows.

15 Therefore I came out to meet you,
    diligently to seek your face, and I have found you.

16 I have decked my bed with coverings of tapestry,
    with carved works, with fine linen of Egypt.

17 I have perfumed my bed
    with myrrh, aloes, and cinnamon.

18 Come, let us take our fill of love until the morning;
    let us solace ourselves with love.

19 For my husband is not at home;
    he has gone on a long journey;

20 he has taken a bag of money with him,
    and will come home at the day appointed."

21 With her enticing speech she caused him to yield,
    with the flattering of her lips she seduced him.

22 He went after her straightway,
    as an ox goes to the slaughter,
    or as a fool to the correction of the stocks,

23 until a dart struck through his liver.
    As a bird hastens to the snare,
    he did not know that it would cost him his life.

24 Listen to me now therefore, O children,
    and attend to the words of my mouth:

25 do not let your heart turn aside to her ways,
    do not go astray in her paths;

26 for she has cast down many wounded,
    and many strong men have been slain by her.

27 Her house is the way to Sheol,
   going down to the chambers of death.

v.7-8 What you do not know can hurt you! Because the youth did not have an understanding that he could call his own, he blindly walked down a road that led to nowhere good. That is why every experience in life is a lesson, if the lesson did not trip you up then you should try to prevent the person behind you from tripping over that lesson.

v.15 Trouble is good friends with simple minded folks. If you do not purpose to avoid trouble it will find you. Like the Venus Fly Trap plant waits for a simple minded bug, the woman was waiting to take advantage of the young man. Trouble found a free meal, and the free meal thought that he was being invited to a dinner party. The young man was receiving an invitation for a free meal...but he was going to be the main course!

Chapter 8:

The Virtue of Wisdom

1 Does not wisdom cry out,
   and understanding lift up her voice?

2 She stands on the top of high places,
   by the way in the places of the paths.

3 She cries out at the gates,
   at the entry of the city, at the entrance of the doors:

4 "To you, O men, I call,
   and my voice is to the sons of men.

5 O you simple, understand wisdom,
   and you fools, be of an understanding heart.

6 Hear, for I will speak of excellent things,
   and from the opening of my lips will be right things;

7 for my mouth will speak truth,
   and wickedness is an abomination to my lips.

8 All the words of my mouth are in righteousness;
   there is nothing crooked or perverse in them.

9 They are all plain to him who understands,
   and right to those who find knowledge.

10 Receive my instruction, and not silver,
   and knowledge rather than choice gold;

11 for wisdom is better than rubies,
   and all the things that may be desired are not to be compared to
   it.

12 "I, wisdom, dwell with prudence,
   and find out knowledge and discretion.

13 The fear of the Lord is to hate evil;
   pride and arrogance
   and the evil way and the perverse mouth I hate.

14 Counsel is mine, and sound wisdom;
   I am understanding, I have strength.

15 By me kings reign,
   and princes decree justice.

16 By me princes rule,
   and nobles, even all the judges of the earth.

17 I love those who love me,
   and those who seek me early will find me.

18 Riches and honor are with me,
   yes, enduring riches and righteousness.

19 My fruit is better than gold,
   yes, than fine gold, and my revenue than choice silver.

20 I lead in the way of righteousness,
   in the midst of the paths of justice,

21 that I may cause those who love me to inherit wealth,
   and I will fill their treasuries.

22 "The Lord possessed me in the beginning of His way,
   before His works of old.

23 I was set up from everlasting,
   from the beginning, before there was ever an earth.

24 When there were no depths, I was brought forth,
   when there were no fountains abounding with water.

25 Before the mountains were settled,
   before the hills I was brought forth;

26 while as yet He had not made the earth or the fields,
   or the first dust of the world.

27 When He prepared the heavens, I was there,
   when He drew a circle on the face of the deep,

28 when He established the clouds above,
   when He strengthened the fountains of the deep,

29 when He gave to the sea His decree,

that the waters should not pass His commandment,
when He appointed the foundations of the earth,

30 then I was by Him, as one brought up with Him;
and I was daily His delight,
rejoicing always before Him,

31 rejoicing in the habitable part of His earth,
and my delights were with the sons of men.

32 "Now therefore listen to me, O you children,
for blessed are those who keep my ways.

33 Hear instruction, and be wise,
and do not refuse it.

34 Blessed is the man who hears me,
watching daily at my gates,
waiting at the posts of my doors.

35 For whoever finds me finds life,
and will obtain favor of the Lord;

36 but he who sins against me wrongs his own soul;
all those who hate me love death."

v. 13 *The fear of the Lord is to hate evil; pride and arrogance and the evil way and the perverse mouth I hate.* Verse 13 further explains the thought that was stated in Proverbs 1:7 *The fear of the Lord is the beginning of knowledge, but fools despise wisdom and instruction.* If you want to start living more wisely then you need to develop a negative outlook to a sinful lifestyle, because sin and Wisdom go together like oil and water.

v. 22-31 If life was to be spoken of like it was a building then Wisdom would be the foundation. Even before the earth was created GOD created Wisdom. Knowing that Wisdom is the ability to recognize difference, it is interesting that GOD established Wisdom before HE created anything on earth. If GOD established Wisdom to be the foundation that the world sits on, then each of us would do well to build our lives with Wisdom as the foundation.

Chapter 9:

The Way of Wisdom

1 Wisdom has built her house,
   she has hewn out her seven pillars;

2 she has killed her beasts, she has mixed her wine,
   she has also furnished her table.

3 She has sent out her maidens,
   she cries out from the highest places of the city,

4 "Whoever is simple, let him turn in here."
   As for him who wants understanding, she says to him,

5 "Come, eat of my bread,
   and drink of the wine which I have mixed.

6 Forsake foolishness and live,
   and go in the way of understanding."

7 He who reproves a scorner gets shame for himself,
   and he who rebukes a wicked man gets hurt.

8 Do not reprove a scorner, lest he hate you;
   rebuke a wise man, and he will love you.

9 Give instruction to a wise man, and he will be yet wiser;
   teach a just man, and he will increase in learning.

10 The fear of the Lord is the beginning of wisdom,
   and the knowledge of the Holy One is understanding.

11 For by me your days will be multiplied,
   and the years of your life will be increased.

12 If you are wise, you will be wise for yourself,
   but if you scorn, you alone will bear it.

The Way of Foolishness

13 A foolish woman is clamorous;
   she is simple, and knows nothing.

14 For she sits at the door of her house,
   on a seat in the high places of the city,

15 to call those who pass by
   who go right on their way:

16 "Whoever is simple, let him turn in here."
   And as for him who lacks understanding, she says to him,

17 "Stolen waters are sweet,
   and bread eaten in secret is pleasant."

18 But he does not know that the dead are there,
   and that her guests are in the depths of the grave.

v. 3 What is being described is not just poetry. In the ancient culture the highest place in the city was reserved as a position of prominence. Wisdom sits on the highest place in the city, and in verse 14 we learn that lady folly who is an imposter that has managed to sit on an elevated place, she is trying to entice the simple minded. Without knowledge and understanding a person might mistake the woman that is named folly for Wisdom. Often times wrong decisions masquerade as good decisions.

v. 5-6 when we read verse 5 and verse 6 it is important to realize that Wisdom is not just inviting us to follow her, but the wise lifestyle will prevent us from making unwise decisions. I am reminded of a line from my favorite book in the Bible Ecclesiastes 2:13 *And I realized that there is an advantage to wisdom over folly, like the advantage of light over darkness.* Ecclesiastes 2:14 further explains that the wise person is like someone that walks around with the ability to see, however the foolish person is not even aware that they are about to stumble into a pit.

v. 1-12 Wisdom has spent time preparing Her home for visitors, She has made ready a giant banquet and to top it all off she has started mass mailing campaigns and has done alot of things to make Her message known. The truth is that often people do not live wisely simply because they do not want to listen to the voice of Wisdom.

Chapter 10:

1 A wise son makes a glad father,
   but a foolish son is the grief of his mother.

2 Treasures of wickedness profit nothing,
   but righteousness delivers from death.

3 The Lord will not allow the soul of the righteous to famish,
   but He casts away the desire of the wicked.

4 He becomes poor who deals with a slack hand,
   but the hand of the diligent makes rich.

5 He who gathers in summer is a wise son,
   but he who sleeps in harvest is a son who causes shame.

6 Blessings are on the head of the just,
   but violence covers the mouth of the wicked.

7 The memory of the just is blessed,
   but the name of the wicked will rot.

8 The wise in heart will receive commandments,
   but a prating fool will fall.

9 He who walks uprightly walks surely,
   but he who perverts his ways will be known.

10 He who winks with the eye causes sorrow,
    but a prating fool will fall.

11 The mouth of a righteous man is a well of life,
    but violence covers the mouth of the wicked.

12 Hatred stirs up strife,
    but love covers all sins.

13 In the lips of him who has understanding wisdom is found,
    but a rod is for the back of him who is void of understanding.

14 Wise men store up knowledge,
    but the mouth of the foolish is near destruction.

15 The rich man's wealth is his strong city;
    the destruction of the poor is their poverty.

16 The labor of the righteous tends to life,
    the fruit of the wicked to sin.

17 He who keeps instruction is in the way of life,
   but he who refuses reproof errs.

18 He who hides hatred has lying lips,
   and he who spreads slander is a fool.

19 In the multitude of words sin is not lacking,
   but he who restrains his lips is wise.

20 The tongue of the just is as choice silver;
   the heart of the wicked is worth little.

21 The lips of the righteous feed many,
   but fools die for lack of wisdom.

22 The blessing of the Lord makes rich,
   and He adds no sorrow with it.

23 To do mischief is like sport to a fool,
   but a man of understanding has wisdom.

24 The fear of the wicked will come upon him,
   but the desire of the righteous will be granted.

25 As the whirlwind passes, so is the wicked no more,
   but the righteous has an everlasting foundation.

26 As vinegar to the teeth and as smoke to the eyes,
   so is the sluggard to those who send him.

27 The fear of the Lord prolongs days,
   but the years of the wicked will be shortened.

28 The hope of the righteous will be gladness,
   but the expectation of the wicked will perish.

29 The way of the Lord is strength to the upright,
   but destruction will come to the workers of iniquity.

30 The righteous will never be removed,
   but the wicked will not inhabit the earth.

31 The mouth of the just brings forth wisdom,
   but the perverse tongue will be cut out.

32 The lips of the righteous know what is acceptable,
   but the mouth of the wicked speaks what is perverse.

< In Proverbs 10:1 – Proverbs 22:16 we enter into a section of the book that uses a style of composition that has not yet been used in the book. In this section we see 375 verses that all use similar types of Hebrew poetry. In English poetry the emphasis is placed on rhyme and meter, but in Hebrew poetry verses are grouped together based off of a similar thought or idea. So in English poetry a lot of attention is placed on the idea that the poem should sound nice and usually poetry is 'graded' by how well the words sound together. However in Hebrew poetry the auditory aspect is not the goal, instead words are grouped together based off the ideas that they convey.

When looking at the 'block' of 375 verses a person might find various literary devices being used, however generally 1 of 3 types of parallelism is used to send the message.

- Synonymous Parallelism

This is a feature where the second line repeats the thought of the first line but in different words. The repetition intensifies the thoughts and feelings being expressed.

> **"A false witness will not go unpunished,**
>
> **And he who speaks lies will not escape"** (Proverbs 19:5).

- Antithetic Parallelism

In this feature the second line is the opposite of the first. In the book of Proverbs, this type of construction the most common of the different types.

"He who keeps the commandment keeps his soul,

But he who is careless of his ways will die" (Proverbs 19:16).

- Synthetic Parallelism

In this poetic style the second line advances the thought of the first. Each line is synonymous but each additional line adds to the thought of the first making it more specific.

"The discretion of a man makes him slow to anger,

And his glory is to overlook a transgression" (Proverbs 19:11).

Chapter 11:

1 The Lord detests dishonest scales,
  but accurate weights find favor with him.

2 When pride comes, then comes disgrace,
  but with humility comes wisdom.

3 The integrity of the upright guides them,
  but the unfaithful are destroyed by their duplicity (deceitfulness, double-dealing).

4 Wealth is worthless in the day of wrath,
  but righteousness delivers from death.

5 The righteousness of the blameless makes their paths straight,
   but the wicked are brought down by their own wickedness.

6 The righteousness of the upright delivers them,
   but the unfaithful are trapped by evil desires.

7 Hopes placed in mortals die with them;
   all the promise of their power comes to nothing.

8 The righteous person is rescued from trouble,
   and it falls on the wicked instead.

9 With their mouths (physical actions) the godless destroy their neighbors,
   but through knowledge the righteous escape.

10 When the righteous prosper, the city rejoices;
   when the wicked perish, there are shouts of joy.

11 Through the blessing of the upright a city is exalted,
   but by the mouth of the wicked it is destroyed.

12 Whoever derides (mocks) their neighbor has no sense,
   but the one who has understanding holds their tongue.

13 A gossip betrays a confidence,
   but a trustworthy person keeps a secret.

14 For lack of guidance a nation falls,
   but victory is won through many advisers.

15 Whoever puts up security for a stranger will surely suffer,
   but whoever refuses to shake hands in pledge is safe.

16 A kindhearted woman gains honor,
   but ruthless men gain only wealth. (The sexes of the individuals could easily be interchanged.)

17 Those who are kind benefit themselves,
   but the cruel bring ruin on themselves.

18 A wicked person earns deceptive wages,
   but the one who sows righteousness reaps a sure reward.

19 Truly the righteous attain life,
   but whoever pursues evil finds death.

20 The Lord detests those whose hearts are perverse,
   but he delights in those whose ways are blameless.

21 Be sure of this: The wicked will not go unpunished,
   but those who are righteous will go free.

22 Like a gold ring in a pig's snout
   is a beautiful woman who shows no discretion.

23 The desire of the righteous ends only in good,
   but the hope of the wicked only in wrath.

24 One person gives freely, yet gains even more;
   another withholds unduly, but comes to poverty.

25 A generous person will prosper;
   whoever refreshes others will be refreshed.

26 People curse the one who hoards grain,
   but they pray God's blessing on the one who is willing to sell.

27 Whoever seeks good finds favor,
   but evil comes to one who searches for it.

28 Those who trust in their riches will fall,
   but the righteous will thrive like a green leaf.

29 Whoever brings ruin on their family will inherit only wind,
   and the fool will be servant to the wise.

30 The fruit of the righteous is a tree of life,
   and the one who is wise saves lives.

31 If the righteous receive their due on earth,
   how much more the ungodly and the sinner!

<verse 4 *Riches do no profit in the day of wrath, but righteousness delivers from death.* It is easy to think that this verse is talking about material wealth, but what is being discussed is a lifestyle that is valuable (a lifestyle that leaves behind a godly legacy.) Both 'the day of wrath' and 'being delivered from death' are speaking of the conclusion of our earthly life. And on that day its really not going to matter how large your investment portfolio was. So if you think that the purpose of life is to live for your self...that is an incorrect thought.

verse 7 *Hopes placed in mortals die with them, all the promise of their power comes to nothing.* At the end of the day then the score will be tallied and all of the so called accomplishments of mankind will amount to nothing.

verse 9 points to what is going to be said in Proverbs 25:21-22 *If your enemy is hungry, give him bread to eat; and if he is thirsty, give him water to drink; 22 for you will heap coals of fire upon his head, and the Lord will reward you.* People that do not spend time learning how GOD wants us to live, they try to speak the worst words to people that they do not like (and thoes words can really mess someone's life up). But GOD tells us that if we meet the individuals needs then HE will vindicate the righteous.

Chapter 12:

1 Whoever loves instruction loves knowledge,
   but he who hates reproof is brutish.

2 A good man obtains favor of the Lord,
   but a man of wicked devices will He condemn.

3 A man will not be established by wickedness,
   but the root of the righteous will not be moved.

4 A virtuous woman is a crown to her husband,
   but she who brings shame is as rottenness in his bones.

5 The thoughts of the righteous are right,
   but the counsels of the wicked are deceit.

6 The words of the wicked are, "Lie in wait for blood,"
   but the mouth of the upright will deliver them.

7 The wicked are overthrown, and are not,
   but the house of the righteous will stand.

8 A man will be commended according to his wisdom,
   but he who is of a perverse heart will be despised.

9 He who is lightly esteemed and has a servant is better
   than he who honors himself and lacks bread.

10 A righteous man regards the life of his animal,
   but the tender mercies of the wicked are cruel.

11 He who tills his land will be satisfied with bread,
   but he who follows vain persons is void of understanding.

12 The wicked covet the plunder of evil men,
   but the root of the righteous yields fruit.

13 The wicked is snared by the transgression of his lips,
   but the just will come out of trouble.

14 A man will be satisfied with good by the fruit of his mouth,
   and the recompense of a man's hands will be rendered to him.

15 The way of a fool is right in his own eyes,
   but he who listens to counsel is wise.

16 A fool's wrath is presently known,
   but a prudent man covers shame.

17 He who speaks truth shows forth righteousness,
   but a false witness deceit.

18 There is one who speaks like the piercings of a sword,
   but the tongue of the wise is health.

19 The truthful lip will be established forever,
   but a lying tongue is but for a moment.

20 Deceit is in the heart of those who imagine evil,
   but to the counselors of peace is joy.

21 There will no evil happen to the just,
   but the wicked will be filled with mischief.

22 Lying lips are abomination to the Lord,
   but those who deal truly are His delight.

23 A prudent man conceals knowledge,
   but the heart of fools proclaims foolishness.

24 The hand of the diligent will rule,
   but the slothful will be put to forced labor.

25 Heaviness in the heart of man makes it droop,
   but a good word makes it glad.

26 The righteous is a guide to his neighbors,
   but the way of the wicked leads them astray.

27 The slothful man does not roast that which he took in hunting,
   but the substance of a diligent man is precious.

28 In the way of righteousness is life,
   and in its pathway there is no death.

v.16 *A fool's wrath is presently known, but a prudent man covers shame.* Verse 16 is somewhat related to v.23 *A prudent man conceals knowledge, but the heart of fools proclaims foolishness.* Both verses reinforce the idea that it is not prudent to express every opinion that you have, instead wait for the proper time and place to have a discussion.

Chapter 13:

1 A wise son heeds his father's instruction,
   but a scoffer does not listen to rebuke.

2 A man will eat well by the fruit of his mouth,
   but the soul of the transgressor will eat violence.

3 He who guards his mouth preserves his life,
   but he who opens wide his lips will have destruction.

4 The soul of the sluggard desires, and has nothing;
   but the soul of the diligent will be made fat.

5 A righteous man hates lying,
   but a wicked man is loathsome and comes to shame.

6 Righteousness keeps him who is upright in the way,
  but wickedness overthrows the sinner.

7 There is one who makes himself rich, yet has nothing;
  there is one who makes himself poor, yet has great riches.

  (There are poor people that pretend to be rich, and there are rich
  people that pretend to be poor.)

8 The ransom of a man's life is his riches,
  but the poor does not hear rebuke.

9 The light of the righteous rejoices,
  but the lamp of the wicked will be put out.

10 Only by pride comes contention,
   but with the well-advised is wisdom.

11 Wealth gained by vanity will be diminished,
   but he who gathers by labor will increase.

12 Hope deferred makes the heart sick,
   but when the desire comes, it is a tree of life.

13 Whoever despises the word will be destroyed,
   but he who fears the commandment will be rewarded.

14 The teaching of the wise is a fountain of life,
   to depart from the snares of death.

15 Good understanding gives favor,
   but the way of transgressors is hard.

16 Every prudent man deals with knowledge,
   but a fool lays open his folly.

17 A wicked messenger falls into mischief,
   but a faithful envoy is health.

18 Poverty and shame will be to him who refuses instruction,
   but he who regards reproof will be honored.

19 The desire accomplished is sweet to the soul,
   but it is abomination to fools to depart from evil.

20 He who walks with wise men will be wise,
   but a companion of fools will be destroyed.

21 Evil pursues sinners,
   but to the righteous good will be repaid.

22 A good man leaves an inheritance to his children's children,
   and the wealth of the sinner is laid up for the just.

23 Much food (advancement) is in the tillage (soil that can be tilled)
   of the poor,
   but for lack of justice it is destroyed.

24 He who spares his rod hates his son,
   but he who loves him disciplines him early.

[The person that Loves (the other person) will point out the correct
   path (even if the guidance is not easy to except). The opportune
   time to do this is as soon as possible.]

25 The righteous eats to the satisfying of his soul,
   but the stomach of the wicked will want.

v. 1. The term 'son' is used in a wide sense. The Hebrew word that is
used is derived from the word **banah** and the word refers to the common builders of the family name, in the widest sense (of literal and
figurative relationship, including grandson, subject, nation, quality or
condition. Basicly the book of Proverbs is referring to people that strive

to live a prudent lifestyle as belonging to a similar clan. So this verse is not just referring to to two people that are biologically related, the term that is being used is more in the realm of an adoptive role model that is sharing advice with someone else that is in his or her clan.

v. 2. Verse 2 reminds me of what is said in Luke 6:45 *"A good man out of the good treasure of his heart bears what is good, and an evil man out of the evil treasure of his heart bears what is evil. For of the abundance of the heart his mouth speaks."*

v. 7. Verse 7 reminds us humans should stop putting so much emphases on the outward appearances of people. Sometimes it is easy to spot the bad apples in life, but sometimes we are looking at talented actors.

v. 19. *"The desire accomplished is sweet to the soul, but it is abomination to fools to depart from evil"* Its easy for people to say that they want things to change but the foolish person does not want to forsake there misguided ways.

v. 22. The verse begins by reminding us that the wise person spends there time building a legacy that they can pass on to future generations, but the only thing that foolish people are able to leave behind is earthly possessions.

v. 23. So its up to us to live our lives in such a way that injustice can not stand to be around us. While reading through Proverbs a person realizes that a large bank account does not automatically make someone rich. Only the Godly person can have riches that can not be taken away.

Chapter 14:

1 Every wise woman builds her house,
  but the foolish pulls it down with her hands.

2 He who walks in his uprightness fears the Lord,
  but he who is perverse in his ways despises Him.

3 In the mouth of the foolish is a rod of pride,
  but the lips of the wise will preserve them.

4 Where no oxen are, the crib is clean;
  but much increase is by the strength of the ox.

5 A faithful witness will not lie,
  but a false witness will utter lies.

6 A scorner seeks wisdom and does not find it,
  but knowledge is easy to him who understands.

7 Go from the presence of a foolish man,
  when you do not perceive in him the lips of knowledge.

8 The wisdom of the prudent is to understand his way,
  but the folly of fools is deceit.

9 Fools make a mock at sin,
  but among the righteous there is favor.

10 The heart knows its own bitterness,
  and a stranger does not share its joy.

11 The house of the wicked will be overthrown,
  but the tent of the upright will flourish.

12 There is a way that seems right to a man,
  but its end is the way of death.

13 Even in laughter the heart is sorrowful,
  and the end of that cheer is grief.

14 The backslider in heart will be filled with his own ways,
  but a good man will be satisfied with his.

15 The simple believes every word,
   but the prudent man considers his steps.

16 A wise man fears and departs from evil,
   but the fool rages and is self-confident.

17 He who is quick-tempered deals foolishly,
   and a man of wicked devices is hated.

18 The simple inherit folly,
   but the prudent are crowned with knowledge.

19 The evil bow before the good,
   and the wicked at the gates of the righteous.

20 The poor is hated even by his own neighbor,
   but the rich has many friends.

21 He who despises his neighbor sins,
   but he who has mercy on the poor, happy is he.

22 Do they not err who devise evil?
   But mercy and truth will be to those who devise good.

23 In all labor there is profit,
   but mere talk leads only to poverty.

24 The crown of the wise is their riches,
   but the foolishness of fools is folly.

25 A true witness delivers souls,
   but a deceitful witness speaks lies.

26 In the fear of the Lord is strong confidence,
   and His children will have a place of refuge.

27 The fear of the Lord is a fountain of life,
   to depart from the snares of death.

28 In the multitude of people is a king's honor,
   but in the lack of people is the destruction of a prince.

29 He who is slow to wrath is of great understanding,
   but he who is hasty of spirit exalts folly.

30 A sound heart is the life of the flesh,
   but envy the rottenness of the bones.

31 He who oppresses the poor reproaches his Maker,
   but he who honors Him has mercy on the poor.

32 The wicked is driven away in his wickedness,
   but the righteous has hope in his death.

33 Wisdom rests in the heart of him who has understanding,
   but that which is in the midst of fools is made known.

34 Righteousness exalts a nation,
   but sin is a reproach to any people.

35 The king's favor is toward a wise servant,
   but his wrath is against him who causes shame.

v. 1. This verse should probably be interpreted as saying *"The Wise Woman"* Or rather, people that are associated with 'The Wise Woman', so 'people that are Wise live in such a way that builds their house (legacy) up...but people that lack Wisdom do not build anything of value (see Proverbs 13:22)

v. 6. *A scorner seeks wisdom and does not find it, but knowledge is easy to him who understands.* The scorner seeks Wisdom and does not find it because GOD hides Wisdom from the scorner (1 Peter 5:5 ...GOD resists the proud but shows favor to the humble.) Why is knowledge easy to the person that understands? Psalms chapter 91 is a beautiful chapter that explains the special relationship that GOD has with the people that Fear HIS NAME and are covered under the BLOOD of GOD's SON JESUS.

Chapter 15:

1 A soft answer turns away wrath,
   but grievous words stir up anger.

2 The tongue of the wise uses knowledge aright,
   but the mouth of fools pours out foolishness.

3 The eyes of the Lord are in every place,
   keeping watch on the evil and the good.

4 A wholesome tongue is a tree of life,
   but perverseness in it crushes the spirit.

5 A fool despises his father's instruction,
   but he who regards reproof is prudent.

6 In the house of the righteous is much treasure,
   but in the revenue of the wicked is trouble.

7 The lips of the wise disperse knowledge,
   but the heart of the foolish does not do so.

8 The sacrifice of the wicked is an abomination to the Lord,
   but the prayer of the upright is His delight.

9 The way of the wicked is an abomination unto the Lord,
   but He loves him who follows after righteousness.

10 Correction is grievous to him who forsakes the way,
   and he who hates reproof will die.

11 Death and destruction are before the Lord;
   so how much more the hearts of the children of men.

12 A scorner does not love one who reproves him,
   nor will he go to the wise.

13 A merry heart makes a cheerful countenance,
   but by sorrow of the heart the spirit is broken.

14 The heart of him who has understanding seeks knowledge,
   but the mouth of fools feeds on foolishness.

15 All the days of the afflicted are evil,
   but he who is of a merry heart has a continual feast.

16 Better is little with the fear of the Lord
   than great treasure with trouble.

17 Better is a dinner of herbs where love is
   than a fatted calf with hatred.

18 A wrathful man stirs up strife,
   but he who is slow to anger appeases strife.

19 The way of the slothful man is as a hedge of thorns,
   but the way of the righteous is made plain.

20 A wise son makes a father glad,
   but a foolish man despises his mother.

21 Folly is joy to him who is destitute of wisdom,
   but a man of understanding walks uprightly.

22 Without counsel, purposes are disappointed,
   but in the multitude of counselors they are established.

23 A man has joy by the answer of his mouth,
   and a word spoken in due season, how good it is!

24 The way of life leads above for the wise,
   that he may depart from Sheol below.

25 The Lord will destroy the house of the proud,
   but He will establish the border of the widow.

26 The thoughts of the wicked are an abomination to the Lord,
   but the words of the pure are pleasant words.

27 He who is greedy of gain troubles his own house,
   but he who hates bribes will live.

28 The heart of the righteous studies to answer,
   but the mouth of the wicked pours out evil things.

29 The Lord is far from the wicked,
   but He hears the prayer of the righteous.

30 The light of the eyes rejoices the heart,
   and a good report makes the bones healthy.

31 The ear that hears the reproof of life
   abides among the wise.

32 He who refuses instruction despises his own soul,
   but he who hears reproof gains understanding.

33 The fear of the Lord is the instruction of wisdom,
   and before honor is humility.

< v.1 Humans tend to imitate what is around them. The other person might be shouting at you because you are shouting at them...so try to deflate the situation and be more gentle. Some people just want to be involved in a shouting match, so deny the other person pleasure

and do not shout back at them. Not many people want to be the only person that is yelling :)

< v.5 A lot can be said about how a person handles correction. Like Henery Ford said "...the airplane takes off against the wind..." The ignorant person scoffs at prudent advice, sometimes constructive criticism can be a good thing. <also verse 12>

Chapter 16:

1 The preparations of the heart belong to man,
  but the answer of the tongue is from the Lord.

2 All the ways of a man are clean in his own eyes,
  but the Lord weighs the spirit.

3 Commit your works to the Lord,
  and your thoughts will be established.

4 The Lord has made all things for Himself,
  yes, even the wicked for the day of evil.

5 Everyone who is proud in heart is an abomination to the Lord;
  be assured, he will not be unpunished.

6 By mercy and truth iniquity is purged;
  and by the fear of the Lord men depart from evil.

7 When a man's ways please the Lord,
  He makes even his enemies to be at peace with him.

8 Better is a little with righteousness
  than great revenues with injustice.

9 A man's heart devises his way,
  but the Lord directs his steps.

10 A divine sentence is in the lips of the king;
   his mouth does not transgress in judgment.

11 A just weight and balance belong to the Lord;
   all the weights of the bag are His work.

12 It is an abomination to kings to commit wickedness,
   for the throne is established by righteousness.

13 Righteous lips are the delight of kings,
   and they love him who speaks right.

14 The wrath of a king is as messengers of death,
   but a wise man will pacify it.

15 In the light of the king's countenance is life,
   and his favor is as a cloud of the latter rain.

16 How much better to get wisdom than gold!
   And to get understanding is to be chosen rather than silver!

17 The highway of the upright is to depart from evil;
   he who keeps his way preserves his soul.

18 Pride goes before destruction,
   and a haughty spirit before a fall.

19 Better it is to be of a humble spirit with the lowly
   than to divide the spoil with the proud.

20 He who handles a matter wisely will find good,
   and whoever trusts in the Lord, happy is he.

21 The wise in heart will be called prudent,
   and the sweetness of the lips increases learning.

22 Understanding is a wellspring of life to him who has it,
   but the instruction of fools is folly.

23 The heart of the wise teaches his mouth,
   and adds learning to his lips.

24 Pleasant words are as a honeycomb,
   sweet to the soul and health to the bones.

25 There is a way that seems right to a man,
   but its end is the way of death.

26 He who labors, labors for himself,
   for his mouth craves it of him.

27 An ungodly man digs up evil,
   and in his lips there is as a burning fire.

28 A perverse man sows strife,
   and a whisperer separates the best of friends.

29 A violent man entices his neighbor,
   and leads him into the way that is not good.

30 He shuts his eyes to devise perverse things;
   moving his lips he brings evil to pass.

31 The gray-haired head is a crown of glory,
   if it is found in the way of righteousness.

32 He who is slow to anger is better than the mighty,
   and he who rules his spirit than he who takes a city.

33 The lot is cast into the lap,
   but the whole outcome is of the Lord.

v.2 Most people think that they are decent people. When most individuals describe themselves they usually do not describe themselves as total reprobates or even rotten. But take a look at the world that we live in! The world is the offspring of people that think that they are 'jolly to be around'. The word for that is deceived! Mankind is deceived into thinking that they are not that bad. Like it says in the book of Jeremiah, this world needs to be rebuilt on a foundation of godly principals

Jeremiah 17:9

The heart is deceitful above all things, and desperately sick; who can understand it?

< v.4 *The Lord has made all things for Himself, yes, even the wicked for the day of evil.* You read that correctly while the wicked person might think that he/she is getting away with something, that person is only reaffirming to GOD the motivations that are in their heart.

Proverbs 17

1 Better is a dry morsel with quietness
   than a house full of sacrifices with strife.

2 A wise servant will have rule over a son who causes shame,
   and will have part of the inheritance among the brothers.

3 The refining pot is for silver and the furnace for gold,
   but the Lord tries the hearts.

4 A wicked doer gives heed to false lips,
   and a liar gives ear to a wayward tongue.

5 Whoever mocks the poor reproaches his Maker,
   and he who is glad at calamities will not be unpunished.

6 Grandchildren are the crown of old men,
   and the glory of children are their fathers.

7 Excellent speech is not becoming to a fool,
   much less lying lips to a prince.

8 A gift is as a precious stone in the eyes of him who has it;
   wherever he turns, it prospers.

9 He who covers a transgression seeks love,
   but he who repeats a matter separates friends.

10 A reproof enters deeper into a wise man
   than a hundred stripes into a fool.

11 An evil man seeks only rebellion;
   therefore a cruel messenger will be sent against him.

12 Let a man meet a bear robbed of her cubs
   rather than a fool in his folly.

13 Whoever rewards evil for good,
   evil will not depart from his house.

14 The beginning of strife is as when one lets out water;
   therefore abandon contention before a quarrel starts.

15 He who justifies the wicked, and he who condemns the just,
   both of them are abomination to the Lord.

16 Why is there a price in the hand of a fool to get wisdom,
   seeing he has no heart for it?

17 A friend loves at all times,
   and a brother is born for adversity.

18 A man void of understanding shakes hands,
   and becomes a pledge in the presence of his friend.

19 He loves transgression who loves strife,
   and he who exalts his gate seeks destruction.

20 He who has a deceitful heart finds no good,
   and he who has a perverse tongue falls into mischief.

21 He who fathers a fool does it to his sorrow,
   and the father of a fool has no joy.

22 A merry heart does good like a medicine,
   but a broken spirit dries the bones.

23 A wicked man takes a bribe out of a hidden place
   to pervert the ways of judgment.

24 Wisdom is before him who has understanding,
   but the eyes of a fool are in the ends of the earth.

25 A foolish son is a grief to his father,
   and bitterness to her who bore him.

26 Also to punish the just is not good,
   nor to strike princes for their uprightness.

27 He who has knowledge spares his words,
   and a man of understanding is of an excellent spirit.

28 Even a fool, when he holds his peace, is counted wise;
   and he who shuts his lips is esteemed a man of understanding.

v.3 It's called the cycle of abuse. Bullies usually do not act on there own accord, often bullies lash out and try to steal other people's sense of self worth because someone might have stolen some of their self worth. Logic dictates that a person can replace what was stolen from them by thievery, but that would be like buying a watch that costs 25 cents. The watch might last for a short while, but before you know it you will need to buy another watch. Help put an end to the cycle of abuse and allow GOD to reshape you heart. Do not try to build yourself up by tearing other people down, instead build yourself up by focusing on what GOD says about you! Lets look and see how GOD wants us to treat others by reading Psalms 1:1-4

Psalm 1

1 Blessed is the man who walks not in the counsel of the ungodly, nor stands in the path of sinners, nor sits in the seat of scoffers;

2 but his delight is in the law of the Lord, and in His law he meditates day and night.

3 He will be like a tree planted by the rivers of water, that brings forth its fruit in its season; its leaf will not wither, and whatever he does will prosper.

4 The ungodly are not so, but are like the chaff which the wind drives away.

Proverbs 18

1 He who separates himself seeks his own desire;
he seeks and quarrels against all wisdom.

2 A fool has no delight in understanding,
but in expressing his own heart.

3 When the wicked comes, then comes also contempt,
and with dishonor reproach.

4 The words of a man's mouth are as deep waters,
and the wellspring of wisdom as a flowing brook.

5 It is not good to favor the wicked,
   or to turn aside the righteous in judgment.

6 A fool's lips enter into contention,
   and his mouth calls for flogging.

7 A fool's mouth is his destruction,
   and his lips are the snare of his soul.

8 The words of a talebearer are as wounds,
   and they go down into the innermost parts of the body.

9 He also who is slothful in his work
   is brother to him who is a great waster.

10 The name of the Lord is a strong tower;
    the righteous run into it and are safe.

11 The rich man's wealth is his strong city,
    and as a high wall in his own conceit.

12 Before destruction the heart of man is haughty,
    and before honor is humility.

13 He who answers a matter before he hears it,
    it is folly and shame to him.

14 The spirit of a man will sustain his infirmity,
    but a wounded spirit who can bear?

15 The heart of the prudent gets knowledge,
    and the ear of the wise seeks knowledge.

16 A man's gift makes room for him,
    and brings him before great men.

17 He who is first in his own cause seems just,
    but his neighbor comes and searches him.

18 The lot causes contentions to cease,
   and keeps the mighty ones apart.

19 A brother offended is harder to be won than a strong city,
   and their contentions are like the bars of a castle.

20 A man's stomach will be satisfied with the fruit of his mouth;
   and with the increase of his lips will he be filled.

21 Death and life are in the power of the tongue,
   and those who love it will eat its fruit.

22 Whoever finds a wife finds a good thing,
   and obtains favor of the Lord.

23 The poor *man* uses entreaties,
   but the rich *man* answers roughly.

24 A man who has friends must show himself friendly,
   and there is a friend who sticks closer than a brother.

v. 6 A fool's lips enter into contention, and his mouth calls for flogging.

As we read through the Book of Proverbs it becomes clear that the words are not just sounds. Words are like bricks that can be used to build a mansion or a prison. Similar words are spoken in verse 21 *a Death and life are in the power of the tongue, b and those who love it will eat its fruit.* We have discussed part 'a' of this verse, however I would like to turn our attention to part 'b'. A more direct interpretation of this part of the verse might read -- 'those that live by the sword, die by the sword' also 'the people that have diarrhea of the mouth will face the consequences'. Like we are taught in James 1:19

... let every man be swift to hear, slow to speak, and slow to anger ...

Note: v. 17. *"He who is first in his own cause seems just, but his neighbor comes and searches him."*

While I am writing this there is an advertisement where a *free _____ is offered. The advertisement seems like a good idea, but the truth is the advertisement just seems like a good idea, but just one side of the conversation is being heard. The point is that every conversation has two sides, and the first side more than likely sounds correct. And the story will likely continue to sound correct until more information is discovered. Before you make a decision make sure that you have all of the information. Verse 17 hints at a verse in chapter 25 (verse 2).

Proverbs 19

1 Better is the poor who walks in his integrity
than he who is perverse in his lips and is a fool.

2 Also, it is not good for the soul to be without knowledge,
and he who hastens with his feet sins.

3 The foolishness of man perverts his way,
and his heart frets against the Lord.

4 Wealth makes many friends,
but the poor is separated from his neighbor.

5 A false witness will not be unpunished,
and he who speaks lies will not escape.

6 Many will entreat the favor of the prince,
and every man is a friend to him who gives gifts.

7 All the brothers of the poor hate him;
how much more do his friends go far from him!

He pursues them with words,
yet they abandon him.

8 He who gets wisdom loves his own soul;
he who keeps understanding will find good.

9 A false witness will not be unpunished,
and he who speaks lies will perish.

10 Delight is not seemly for a fool,
much less for a servant to have rule over princes.

11 The discretion of a man defers his anger,
and it is his glory to pass over a transgression.

12 The king's wrath is as the roaring of a lion,
but his favor is as dew upon the grass.

13 A foolish son is the calamity of his father,
and the contentions of a wife are a continual dripping of water.

14 House and riches are the inheritance of fathers,
and a prudent wife is from the Lord.

15 Slothfulness casts into a deep sleep,
and an idle soul will suffer hunger.

16 He who keeps the commandment keeps his own soul,
but he who is careless in his ways will die.

17 He who has pity on the poor lends to the Lord,
and He will repay what he has given.

18 Chasten your son while there is hope,
and let not your soul spare for his crying.

19 A man of great wrath will suffer punishment;
for if you deliver him, yet you must do it again.

20 Hear counsel and receive instruction,
   that you may be wise in your latter days.

21 There are many plans in a man's heart,
   nevertheless the counsel of the Lord will stand.

22 The desire of a man is his kindness,
   and a poor man is better than a liar.

23 The fear of the Lord tends to life,
   and he who has it will abide satisfied; he will not be visited with
   evil.

24 A slothful man hides his hand in his bowl,
   and will not so much as bring it to his mouth again.

25 Smite a scorner, and the simple will beware;
   and reprove one who has understanding, and he will understand
   knowledge.

26 He who mistreats his father and chases away his mother
   is a son who causes shame and brings reproach.

27 Cease, my son, to hear the instruction
   that causes to err from the words of knowledge.

28 An ungodly witness scorns judgment,
   and the mouth of the wicked devours iniquity.

29 Judgments are prepared for scorners,
   and beatings for the back of fools.

v. 3 The culture that we live in today cerebrates the lives of individuals that endure criticism and stand up for a just cause. If I told

people of a man that stood against all odds, and endured severe criticism...eventually laying HIS life down in resistance to a corrupt system. People would want me to strike up the band and to make ready a ticker tape parade! But if I told you that JESUS is the He-man that we are discussing, I am sure that many people would grasp for an eraser giving all manner of excuses to discredit HIS movement. That is exactly what verse 3 is pointing out! The average person would travel a great distance just to avoid modeling there lives after CHRIST and the irony of the situation is that most people would like to stand for truth...however because of a persons pride and arrogance most people will not denounce the lie that is being told. To all of the social justice warriors, you guys think that society will become more 'fair' if you could exclude GOD....your hearts are raging against the LORD!

Proverbs 20

1 Wine is a mocker, strong drink is raging,
   and whoever is deceived by it is not wise.

2 The terror of a king is as the roaring of a lion;
   whoever provokes him to anger sins against his own soul.

3 It is an honor for a man to cease from strife,
   but every fool will be meddling.

4 The sluggard will not plow because of the cold;
   therefore he will beg during harvest and have nothing.

5 Counsel in the heart of man is like deep water,
   but a man of understanding will draw it out.

6 Most men will proclaim everyone his own goodness,
   but who can find a faithful man?

7 The just man walks in his integrity;
   his children are blessed after him.

8 A king who sits on the throne of judgment
   scatters away all evil with his eyes.

9 Who can say, "I have made my heart clean,
   I am pure from my sin"?

10 Diverse weights and diverse measures,
    both of them alike are an abomination to the Lord.

11 Even a child is known by his doings,
    whether his work is pure and whether it is right.

12 The hearing ear and the seeing eye,
    the Lord has made both of them.

13 Do not love sleep, lest you come to poverty;
    open your eyes, and you will be satisfied with bread.

14 "It is bad, it is bad," says the buyer;
    but when he has gone his way, then he boasts.

15 There is gold and a multitude of rubies,
    but the lips of knowledge are a precious jewel.

16 Take the garment of him who is a pledge for a stranger,
    and hold it as a security when it is for a wayward woman.

17 Bread of deceit is sweet to a man,
    but after wards his mouth will be filled with gravel.

18 Every purpose is established by counsel,
    and with good advice wage war.

19 He who goes about as a talebearer reveals secrets;
    therefore do not meddle with him who flatters with his lips.

20 Whoever curses his father or his mother,
   his lamp will be put out in obscure darkness.

21 An inheritance may be gained hastily at the beginning,
   but the end of it will not be blessed.

22 Do not say, "I will recompense evil";
   but wait on the Lord, and He will save you.

23 Diverse weights are an abomination to the Lord,
   and a false balance is not good.

24 Man's goings are of the Lord;
   how can a man then understand his own way?

25 It is a snare to the man who dedicates rashly that which is holy,
   and after the vows to make inquiry.

26 A wise king sifts out the wicked,
   and drives the threshing wheel over them.

27 The spirit of man is the candle of the Lord,
   searching all the inward parts of the heart.

28 Mercy and truth preserve the king,
   and his throne is upheld by mercy.

29 The glory of young men is their strength,
   and the beauty of old men is the gray head.

30 The blows of a wound cleanse away evil,
   so do stripes the inward parts of the heart.

   v. 11 *Even a child is known by his doings, whether his work is pure and whether it is right.* What kind of person expects an apple tree to produce grapes. Verse 11 sounds similar to Mathew 7:16 *You will recognize them by their fruits. Are grapes gathered from thorn bushes, or figs from thistles?*

v. 13 *Do not love sleep, lest you come to poverty; open your eyes, and you will be satisfied with bread.* Much of Proverbs should not be taken only at face value, this verse is not saying that if you never go to sleep then you will have an abundance of food. Verse 13 is a good commentary on verse 4. Verse 13 has little to do with your ability to sleep, instead what is being discussed is an inactive person that is content with doing nothing.

Proverbs 21

1 The king's heart is in the hand of the Lord,
   as the rivers of water; He turns it to any place He will.

2 Every way of a man is right in his own eyes,
   but the Lord weighs the hearts.

3 To do justice and judgment
   is more acceptable to the Lord than sacrifice.

4 A high look, a proud heart,
   and the plowing of the wicked are sin.

5 The thoughts of the diligent tend only to plenty,
   but of everyone who is hasty only to want.

6 The getting of treasures by a lying tongue
   is a vanity tossed back and forth by those who seek death.

7 The violence of the wicked will destroy them,
   because they refuse to do justice.

8 The way of a guilty man is perverse;

but as for the pure, his work is right.

9 It is better to dwell in a corner of the housetop
   than with a brawling woman in a wide house.

10 The soul of the wicked desires evil;
   his neighbor finds no favor in his eyes.

11 When the scorner is punished, the simple is made wise;
   and when the wise is instructed, he receives knowledge.

12 The righteous man wisely considers the house of the wicked,
   but God overthrows the wicked for their wickedness.

13 Whoever shuts his ears at the cry of the poor,
   he also will cry himself, but will not be heard.

14 A gift in secret pacifies anger,
   and a concealed bribe strong wrath.

15 It is joy to the just to do justice,
   but destruction will come to the workers of iniquity.

16 The man who wanders out of the way of understanding
   will remain in the congregation of the dead.

17 He who loves pleasure will be a poor man;
   he who loves wine and oil will not be rich.

18 The wicked will be a ransom for the righteous,
   and the transgressor for the upright.

19 It is better to dwell in the wilderness
   than with a contentious and angry woman.

20 There is treasure to be desired and oil in the dwelling of the wise,
   but a foolish man squanders it.

21 He who follows after righteousness and mercy
   finds life, righteousness, and honor.

22 A wise man scales the city of the mighty,
   and casts down the strength of its confidence.

23 Whoever guards his mouth and his tongue
   keeps his soul from trouble.

24 Proud and haughty—scorner is his name,
   who deals in proud wrath.

25 The desire of the slothful kills him,
   for his hands refuse to labor.

26 He covets greedily all the day long,
   but the righteous gives and does not spare.

27 The sacrifice of the wicked is an abomination;
   how much more when he brings it with a wicked intent!

28 A false witness will perish,
   but a man who listens will speak forever.

29 A wicked man hardens his face,
   but as for the upright, he directs his way.

30 There is no wisdom nor understanding nor counsel
   against the Lord.

31 The horse is prepared against the day of battle,
   but victory is of the Lord.

v.9 *It is better to dwell in a corner of the housetop than with a brawling woman in a wide house.*

A solitary corner, replete with inconveniences, is to be preferred to house shared with woman, wife or other female relation, of a quarrelsome and vexatious temper. Genesis 3:16 explains that women and men do not see things the same way.

v.31 *The horse is prepared against the day of battle, but victory is of the Lord.* Some people never give thought that today could be there last day on this earth. GOD can withdraw every once of strength in that persons body. 'The great truth here taught may be applied to spiritual matters. The only safety against spiritual enemies is the grace of God...' a person can make all sorts of plans, and the wind can blow all of those plans away. A wise person realizes that they should make every preparation (within reason) to succeed, but at the end of the day the outcome is in the hands of the LORD.

Proverbs 22

1 A good name is rather to be chosen than great riches,
   and loving favor rather than silver and gold.

2 The rich and poor have this in common,
   the Lord is the maker of them all.

3 A prudent man foresees the evil and hides himself,
   but the simple pass on and are punished.

4 By humility and the fear of the Lord
   are riches, and honor, and life.

5 Thorns and snares are in the way of the perverse;
   he who guards his soul will be far from them.

6 Train up a child in the way he should go,
   and when he is old he will not depart from it.

7 The rich rules over the poor,
  and the borrower is servant to the lender.

8 He who sows iniquity will reap vanity,
  and the rod of his anger will fail.

9 He who has a bountiful eye will be blessed,
  for he gives of his bread to the poor.

10 Cast out the scorner, and contention will go out;
   yes, strife and reproach will cease.

11 He who loves pureness of heart, for the grace of his lips
   the king will be his friend.

12 The eyes of the Lord preserve knowledge,
   and He overthrows the words of the transgressor.

13 The slothful man says, "There is a lion without (outside)!
   I will be slain in the streets!" (A slothful person has an excuse for
   everything.)

14 The mouth of an immoral woman is a deep pit;
   he who is detested by the Lord will fall therein.

15 Foolishness is bound in the heart of a child,
   but the rod of correction will drive it far from him.

16 He who oppresses the poor to increase his riches,
   and he who gives to the rich, will surely come to want.

-Thirty Sayings of the Wise-

Saying One

17 Incline your ear and hear the words of the wise,
   and apply your heart to my knowledge;

18 for it is a pleasant thing if you keep them within you;
   they will readily be fitted in your lips.

19 That your trust may be in the Lord,
   I have made known to you this day, even to you.

20 Have I not written to you excellent things
   in counsels and knowledge,

21 that I might make you know the certainty of the words of truth,
   that you might answer the words of truth
   to those who send to you?

Saying Two

22 Do not rob the poor because he is poor,
   neither oppress the afflicted in the gate;

23 for the Lord will plead their cause,
   and spoil the soul of those who spoiled them.

Saying Three

24 Make no friendship with an angry man,
   and with a furious man you will not go,

25 lest you learn his ways
   and get a snare to your soul.

Saying Four

26 Do not be one of those who shakes hands in a pledge,
   or of those who use securities for debts;

27 if you have nothing to pay,
   why should he take away your bed from under you?

Saying Five

28 Do not remove the ancient landmark
which your fathers have set.

Saying Six

29 Do you see a man diligent in his business?
He will stand before kings;
he will not stand before obscure men.

v. 6-7 *Train up a child in the way he should go, and when he is old he will not depart from it. The rich rules over the poor, and the borrower is servant to the lender.* I think that many people would be in a different position if only someone had explained to them that debt is a form of slavery.

v.13 *The slothful man says, "There is a lion without* (outside)! *I will be slain in the streets!"* (A slothful person has an excuse for everything.) Some people have an excuse for everything. Thoes kinds of people practice self deceit, and thy might become angry if you point out the inconsistencies in there statements. ex. Some people want you to believe that they want to live a lifestyle of fitness but they claim to be to busy, in reality they are busy eating cookies, like I said most people like that do not want to hear you say that the biggest problem that they have is themselves.

Proverbs 23

Saying Seven

1 When you sit to eat with a ruler,
consider diligently what is before you;

2 and put a knife to your throat,
   if you are a man given to appetite.

3 Be not desirous of his delicacies,
   for they are deceptive food.

Saying Eight

4 Do not labor to be rich;
   cease from your own wisdom.

5 Will you set your eyes on that which is not?
   For riches certainly make themselves wings;
   they fly away as an eagle toward heaven.

Saying Nine

6 Do not eat the bread of him who has an evil eye,
   neither desire his delicacies;

7 for as he thinks in his heart,
   so is he.
   "Eat and drink!" he says to you,
   but his heart is not with you.

8 The morsel you have eaten, you will vomit up,
   and lose your sweet words.

Saying Ten

9 Do not speak in the ears of a fool,
   for he will despise the wisdom of your words.

Saying Eleven

10 Do not remove the old landmark,
   nor enter the fields of the fatherless;

11 for their Redeemer is mighty;
   He will plead their cause with you.

Saying Twelve

12 Apply your heart to instruction,
   and your ears to the words of knowledge.

Saying Thirteen

13 Do not withhold correction from a child,
   for if you beat him with the rod, he will not die.

14 You shall beat him with the rod,
   and deliver his soul from death.

Saying Fourteen

15 My son, if your heart is wise,
   my heart will rejoice—even mine.

16 Yes, my inmost being will rejoice
   when your lips speak right things.

Saying Fifteen

17 Do not let your heart envy sinners,
   but continue in the fear of the Lord all day long;

18 for surely there is an end,
   and your expectation will not be cut off.

Saying Sixteen

19 Hear, my son, and be wise;
   and guide your heart in the way.

20 Do not be among winebibbers,
   among riotous eaters of meat;

21 for the drunkard and the glutton will come to poverty,
   and drowsiness will clothe a man with rags.

Saying Seventeen

22 Listen to your father who gave you life,
   and do not despise your mother when she is old.

23 Buy the truth, and do not sell it,
   also wisdom and instruction and understanding.

24 The father of the righteous will greatly rejoice,
   and he who fathers a wise child will have joy of him.

25 Your father and your mother will be glad,
   and she who bore you will rejoice.

Saying Eighteen

26 My son, give me your heart,
   and let your eyes observe my ways.

27 For a prostitute is a deep ditch,
   and a seductress is a narrow pit.

28 She also lies in wait as for a prey,
   and increases the transgressors among men.

Saying Nineteen

29 Who has woe? Who has sorrow?
   Who has contentions? Who has babbling?
   Who has wounds without cause? Who has redness of eyes?

30 Those who tarry long at the wine,
   those who go to seek mixed wine.

31 Do not look on the wine when it is red,
   when it sparkles in the cup,
   when it swirls around smoothly;

32 at the last it bites like a serpent,
   and stings like a viper.

33 Your eyes will see strange things,
   and your heart will utter perverse things.

34 Yes, you will be as he who lies down in the midst of the sea,
   or as he who lies upon the top of a mast.

35 "They have stricken me," you will say, "and I was not sick;
   they have beaten me, and I did not feel it.
   When will I awake?
   I will seek it yet again."

Note: v. 12. *Apply your heart to instruction, and your ears to the words of knowledge.* I would like people to interpret the saying to be a fancy way to say **'Think about it'** Many are the problems in society just because some people fail to think. An example of what I am saying is that some people think that having an abortion should be a personal decision, but those kinds of people do not understand how our financial system works. Abortion is a scourge on the whole of humanity. Some people might be think that part of there earnings are being stashed away in a governmental account that will fund their personal retirement. But the way that it works is the money that they are putting into the account is being spent. Their retirement is supposedly going to be funded by future workers. So the saying 'abortion is a personal choice' is untrue. The facts are that every child/person that is removed from the labor force, the less strong the economy is going to be. I am reminded of the WORDs of The GOD/KING in Haggai 1:7 ...*Consider your ways!*

Proverbs 24

Saying Twenty

1 Do not be envious against evil men,
　　nor desire to be with them;

2 for their heart studies destruction,
　　and their lips talk of mischief.

Saying Twenty-One

3 Through wisdom is a house built,
　　and by understanding it is established;

4 and by knowledge the rooms will be filled
　　with all precious and pleasant riches.

Saying Twenty-Two

5 A wise man is strong;
　　yes, a man of knowledge increases strength.

6 For by wise counsel you will wage your war,
　　and in multitude of counselors there is safety.

Saying Twenty-Three

7 Wisdom is too high for a fool;
　　he does not open his mouth in the gate.

Saying Twenty-Four

8 He who devises to do evil
   will be called a schemer of plots.

9 The thought of foolishness is sin,
   and the scorner is an abomination to men.

Saying Twenty-Five

10 If you faint in the day of adversity,
   your strength is small.

11 If you refrain to deliver those who are drawn unto death,
   and those who are ready to be slain;

12 if you say, "Surely we did not know this,"
   does not He who ponders the heart consider it?
   And He who keeps your soul, does He not know it?
   And will He not render to every man according to his works?

Saying Twenty-Six

13 My son, eat honey because it is good,
   and the honeycomb that is sweet to your taste;

14 so shall the knowledge of wisdom be to your soul;
   when you have found it, then there will be a reward,
   and your expectation will not be cut off.

Saying Twenty-Seven

15 Do not lie in wait, O wicked man, against the dwelling of the righteous;
   do not spoil his resting place;

16 for a just man falls seven times and rises up again,
   but the wicked will fall into mischief.

Saying Twenty-Eight

17 Do not rejoice when your enemy falls,
   and do not let your heart be glad when he stumbles;

18 lest the Lord see it, and it displease Him,
   and He turn away His wrath from him.

Saying Twenty-Nine

19 Do not fret because of evil men,
   nor be envious of the wicked;

20 for there will be no reward to the evil man;
   the candle of the wicked will be put out.

Saying Thirty

21 My son, fear the Lord and the king;
   and do not meddle with those who are given to change;

22 for their calamity will rise suddenly,
   and who knows the ruin of them both?

More Sayings of the Wise

23 These *things* also *belong* to the wise:
   It is not good to show partiality in judgment.

24 He who says to the wicked, "You are righteous,"
   him the people will curse; nations will abhor him.

25 But to those who rebuke him will be delight,
   and a good blessing will come upon them.

26 Every man will kiss his lips
   that gives a right answer.

27 Prepare your work outside,
   and make it fit for yourself in the field;
   and afterwards build your house.

28 Do not be a witness against your neighbor without cause,
   and do not deceive with your lips.
   29 Do not say, "I will do so to him as he has done to me;
   I will render to the man according to his work."

30 I went by the field of the slothful,
   and by the vineyard of the man void of understanding;

31 and it was all grown over with thorns,
   and nettles covered its surface,
   and the stone wall was broken down.

32 Then I saw, and considered it;
   I looked on it and received instruction:

33 Yet a little sleep, a little slumber,
   a little folding of the hands to sleep,

34 so your poverty will come like a stalker,
   and your need as an armed man.

verse 29 *Do not say, "I will do so to him as he has done to me; I will render to the man according to his work."* This verse is not encouraging people to be societies doormats. This verse is speaking to the people that constantly treat others in a cold hearted manner. Some people just have an ax to grind, and they are not interested in

seeing a matter resolved. Some people only want to see someone else hurt...people like that are said to be 'only interested in blood'. That is a dangerous mindset for someone to have, and its dangerous to hang around people like that. *<See Proverbs 1:10-15>*

Proverbs 25

1 These are also proverbs of Solomon, which the men of Hezekiah king of Judah copied.

2 It is the glory of God to conceal a thing,
but the honor of kings is to search out a matter.

3 As the heaven for height, and the earth for depth,
so the heart of kings is unsearchable.

4 Take away the dross from the silver,
and there will come forth a vessel for the refiner.

5 Take away the wicked from before the king,
and his throne will be established in righteousness.

6 Do not exalt yourself in the presence of the king,
and do not stand in the place of great men;

7 for it is better that it be said to you, "Come up here,"
than that you should be put lower in the presence of the prince,
whom your eyes have seen.

8 Do not go forth hastily to strive;
lest you do not know what to do in the end,
when your neighbor has put you to shame.

9 Debate your cause with your neighbor himself,
and do not disclose a secret to another;

10 lest he who hears it put you to shame,
   and your reputation be ruined.

11 A word fitly spoken
   is like apples of gold in settings of silver.

12 As an earring of gold and an ornament of fine gold,
   so is a wise reprover to an obedient ear.

13 As the cold of snow in the time of harvest,
   so is a faithful messenger to those who send him,
   for he refreshes the soul of his masters.

14 Whoever boasts himself of a false gift
   is like clouds and wind without rain.

15 By long forbearing is a prince persuaded,
   and a soft tongue breaks the bone.

16 Have you found honey? Eat only as much as is sufficient for you,
   lest you be filled with it and vomit it.

17 Withdraw your foot from your neighbor's house,
   lest he be weary of you and so hate you.

18 A man who bears false witness against his neighbor
   is like a club, a sword, and a sharp arrow.

19 Confidence in an unfaithful man in time of trouble
   is like a broken tooth and a foot out of joint.

20 As he who takes away a garment in cold weather,
   and as vinegar on soda,
   so is he who sings songs to a heavy heart.

21 If your enemy is hungry, give him bread to eat;
   and if he is thirsty, give him water to drink;

22 for you will heap coals of fire upon his head,
   and the Lord will reward you.

23 The north wind brings rain,
   and a backbiting tongue an angry countenance.

24 It is better to dwell in the corner of the housetop
   than with a brawling woman in a wide house.

25 As cold waters to a thirsty soul,
   so is good news from a far country.

26 A righteous man falling down before the wicked
   is as a troubled fountain and a corrupt spring.

27 It is not good to eat much honey;
   so for men to search their own glory is not glory.

28 He who has no rule over his own spirit
   is like a city that is broken down and without walls.

Note:

verse 2 *It is the glory of God to conceal a thing, but the honor of kings is to search out a matter.*

In my opinion, GOD seems to LOVE to hide things! It's like GOD LOVES to play a challenging game of 'hide and seek'. The way that I see things life is like a field that GOD has hidden gems in. GOD did not bury all of the valuable gems on the surface. And like Hebrews 11:6 teaches us *"GOD rewards those that diligently seek HIM."* So it works out well, GOD is glorified when HE conceals something, and people that are in authority receive honor when they search a matter out!

verse 9 *Debate your cause with your neighbor himself, and do not disclose a secret to another*

When a dispute arises, the correct way to handle the situation is for the two parties that are involved to civilly discuss the issue and try to reach an agreement. The correct procedure is not to tell everybody about how Jim is not treating you fairly, instead the first thing that you need to do is to speak to Jim.

Proverbs 26

1 As snow in summer, and as rain in harvest,
   so honor is not seemly for a fool.

2 As the bird by flitting, as the swallow by flying,
   so the curse without cause will not alight.

3 A whip for the horse, a bridle for the donkey,
   and a rod for the fool's back.

4 Do not answer a fool according to his folly,
   lest you also be like unto him.

5 Answer a fool according to his folly,
   lest he be wise in his own conceit.

6 He who sends a message by the hand of a fool
   cuts off the feet and drinks violence.

7 The legs of the lame are not equal;
   so is a parable in the mouth of fools.

8 As he who binds a stone in a sling,
   so is he who gives honor to a fool.

9 As a thorn goes into the hand of a drunkard,
   so is a parable in the mouth of fools.

10 The great God who formed all things
   rewards the fool and rewards the transgressor.

11 As a dog returns to its vomit,
   so a fool returns to his folly.

12 Do you see a man wise in his own conceit?
   There is more hope for a fool than for him.

13 The slothful man says, "There is a lion in the way!
   A lion is in the streets!"

14 As the door turns upon his hinges,
   so does the slothful upon his bed.

15 The slothful buries his hand in his bowl;
   it grieves him to bring it again to his mouth.

16 The sluggard is wiser in his own conceit
   than seven men who can answer reasonably.

17 He who passes by and meddles with strife not belonging to him
   is like one who takes a dog by the ears.

18 As a madman who casts
   firebrands, arrows, and death,

19 so is the man who deceives his neighbor,
   and says, "I was only joking."

20 Where there is no wood, the fire goes out;
   so where there is no talebearer, the strife ceases.

21 As charcoal is to burning coals, and wood to fire,
   so is a contentious man to kindle strife.

22 The words of a talebearer are as wounds,
   and go down into the innermost parts of the body.

23 Burning lips and a wicked heart
   are like earthenware covered with silver dross.

24 He who hates dissembles with his lips,
   and lays up deceit within him;

25 when he speaks kindly, do not believe him,
   for there are seven abominations in his heart;

26 though his hatred is covered by deceit,
   his wickedness will be shown before the whole congregation.

27 Whoever digs a pit will fall into it,
   and he who rolls a stone, it will return upon him.

28 A lying tongue hates those who are afflicted by it,
   and a flattering mouth works ruin.

verse 17 *He who passes by and meddles with strife not belonging to him is like one who takes a dog by the ears.*

Verse 17 does not give permission for Kingdomites (that is citizens of The Kingdom of GOD) to ignore the mistreatment of there fellow man, but sometimes people invite trouble into their lives because there noses are a tad to long.

Proverbs 27

1 Do not boast about tomorrow,
   for you do not know what a day may bring forth.

2 Let another man praise you, and not your own mouth;
   a stranger, and not your own lips.

3 A stone is heavy and the sand weighty,
   but a fool's wrath is heavier than them both.

4 Wrath is cruel, and anger is outrageous,
   but who is able to stand before envy?

5 Open rebuke is better
   than secret love.

6 Faithful are the wounds of a friend,
   but the kisses of an enemy are deceitful.

7 The full soul loathes a honeycomb,
   but to the hungry soul every bitter thing is sweet.

8 As a bird that wanders from her nest,
   so is a man who wanders from his place.

9 Ointment and perfume rejoice the heart,
   so does the sweetness of a man's friend by hearty counsel.

10 Do not forsake your own friend or your father's friend,
   nor go into your brother's house in the day of your calamity;
   for better is a neighbor who is near than a brother far off.

11 My son, be wise, and make my heart glad,
   that I may answer him who reproaches me.

12 A prudent man foresees the evil and hides himself,
   but the simple pass on and are punished.

13 Take his garment that is security for a stranger,
   and take a pledge of him for an adulterous woman.

14 He who blesses his friend with a loud voice, rising early in the
   morning,
   it will be counted a curse to him.

15 A continual dripping on a very rainy day
   and a contentious woman are alike;

16 whoever restrains her restrains the wind,
   and grasps oil in his right hand.

17 Iron sharpens iron,
   so a man sharpens the countenance of his friend.

18 Whoever keeps the fig tree will eat its fruit;
   so he who waits on his master will be honored.

19 As in water face answers to face,
   so the heart of man to man.

20 Death and destruction are never full;
   so the eyes of man are never satisfied.

21 As the refining pot for silver, and the furnace for gold,
   so is a man to his praise.

22 Though you should grind a fool in a mortar
   among wheat with a pestle,
   yet his foolishness will not depart from him.

23 Be diligent to know the state of your flocks,
   and look well to your herds;

24 for riches are not forever,
   nor does the crown endure to every generation.

25 The hay appears, and the tender grass shows itself,
   and herbs of the mountains are gathered.

26 The lambs are for your clothing,
   and the goats are the price of the field.

27 You will have goats' milk enough
   for your food, for the food of your household,
   and for the maintenance of your maidens.

verse 1 *Do not boast about tomorrow, for you do not know what a day may bring forth.*

One way to identify a fool is that the habitually spread shady information. Maby you have noticed that this life is extremely fragile, the sun might be shining one moment and the next moment a thunderstorm might pop up.

verse 12 *A prudent man foresees the evil and hides himself, but the simple pass on and are punished.*

A good amount of trouble could be avoided if more people thought ahead. This is illustrated by the phrase that Benjamin Franklin said 'an ounce of prevention is worth a pound of cure'

Proverbs 28

1 The wicked flee when no man pursues,
   but the righteous are bold as a lion.

2 Because of the transgression of a land, many are its princes;
   but by a man of understanding and knowledge, it shall be
   prolonged.

3 A poor man who oppresses the poor
   is like a sweeping rain that leaves no food.

4 Those who forsake instruction praise the wicked,
   but such as keep instruction contend with them.

5 Evil men do not understand justice,
   but those who seek the Lord understand all things.

6 Better is the poor who walks in his uprightness
   than he who is perverse in his ways, though he be rich.

7 Whoever keeps the law is a wise son,
   but he who is a companion of riotous men shames his father.

8 He who by usury and unjust gain increases his substance
   will gather it for him who will pity the poor.

9 He who turns away his ear from hearing instruction,
   even his prayer will be an abomination.

10 Whoever causes the righteous to go astray in an evil way,
    he himself will fall into his own pit;
    but the upright will have good things in possession.

11 The rich man is wise in his own conceit,
    but the poor who has understanding searches him out.

12 When righteous men rejoice, there is great glory;
    but when the wicked rise, a man hides himself.

13 He who covers his sins will not prosper,
    but whoever confesses and forsakes them will have mercy.

14 Happy is the man who always fears <respects his position before
    GOD>,
    but he who hardens his heart will fall into mischief.

15 As a roaring lion and a charging bear,
    so is a wicked ruler over the poor people.

16 The prince who lacks understanding is also a great oppressor,
    but he who hates covetousness will prolong his days.

17 A man burdened with bloodshed of any person
   will flee until death;
   let no man help him.

18 Whoever walks uprightly will be saved,
   but he who is perverse in his ways will fall at once.

19 He who tills his land will have plenty of bread,
   but he who follows after vain things will have poverty enough.

20 A faithful man will abound with blessings,
   but he who makes haste to be rich will not be innocent.

21 To show partiality is not good,
   because for a morsel of bread that man will transgress.

22 He who hastens to be rich has an evil eye,
   and does not consider that poverty will come upon him.

23 He who rebukes a man will find more favor afterward
   than he who flatters with the tongue.

24 Whoever robs his father or his mother
   and says, "It is no transgression,"
   the same is the companion of a destroyer.

25 He who is of a proud heart stirs up strife,
   but he who puts his trust in the Lord will prosper.

26 He who trusts in his own heart is a fool,
   but whoever walks wisely will be delivered.

27 He who gives to the poor will not lack,
   but he who hides his eyes will have many a curse.

28 When the wicked rise, men hide themselves;
   but when they perish, the righteous increase.

verse 9 *He who turns away his ear from hearing instruction, even his prayer will be an abomination.*

Verse 9 is not saying that we need to become like sponges and absorb all the advice that anyone has to say, a good way to get into trouble is to listen to certain people. Instead each of us needs to figure out what the Bible has to say, and if we ignore Biblical instruction even our prayers will not be answered.

Proverbs 29

1 He who is often reproved, yet hardens his neck,
   will suddenly be destroyed, and that without remedy.

2 When the righteous are in authority, the people rejoice;
   but when the wicked rule, the people mourn.

3 Whoever loves wisdom rejoices his father,
   but he who keeps company with harlots spends his substance.

4 The king establishes the land by judgment,
   but he who receives bribes overthrows it.

5 A man who flatters his neighbor
   spreads a net for his feet.

6 In the transgression of an evil man there is a snare,
   but the righteous sing and rejoice.

7 The righteous considers the cause of the poor,
   but the wicked regards not to know it.

8 Scornful men bring a city into a snare,
   but wise men turn away wrath.

9 If a wise man contends with a foolish man,
  whether he rage or laugh, there is no rest.

10 The bloodthirsty hate the upright,
  but the just seek his soul.

11 A fool utters all his mind,
  but a wise man keeps it in until afterwards.

12 If a ruler listens to lies,
  all his servants are wicked.

13 The poor and the deceitful man have this in common:
  The Lord gives light to the eyes of both.

14 The king who faithfully judges the poor,
  his throne will be established forever.

15 The rod and reproof give wisdom,
  but a child left to himself brings his mother to shame.

16 When the wicked are multiplied, transgression increases;
  but the righteous will see their fall.

17 Correct your son, and he will give you rest;
  yes, he will give delight to your soul.

18 Where there is no vision, the people perish;
  but happy is he who keeps the teaching.

19 A servant will not be corrected by words,
  for though he understands he will not answer.

20 Do you see a man who is hasty in his words?
  There is more hope for a fool than for him.

21 He who delicately brings up his servant from a child
  will have him as a son in the end.

22 An angry man stirs up strife,
   and a furious man abounds in transgression.

23 A man's pride will bring him low,
   but honor will uphold the humble in spirit.

24 Whoever is partner with a thief hates his own soul;
   he hears the oath but tells nothing.

25 The fear of man brings a snare,
   but whoever puts his trust in the Lord will be safe.

26 Many seek the ruler's favor,
   but every man's judgment comes from the Lord.

27 An unjust man is an abomination to the just,
   and he who is upright in the way is an abomination to the
   wicked.

verse 12 *If a ruler listens to lies, all his servants are wicked.* I do not know exactly everything that this verse teaches, but just because I only understand part of the verse that does not mean that I can not learn from what it teaches. I understand that if a person that is in authority listens to lies then its not good...so the lesson is 'Do not go along with lies'!

verse 25 *The fear of man brings a snare, but whoever puts his trust in the Lord will be safe.* Verse 25 is not talking about common fear. What verse 25 is pointing out is that if a person thinks that other people are the highest office that they have to answer to...that kind of thinking is a trap! Consider the WORDs of JESUS in Luke 12:4-5 *4 I tell you, MY friends, do not be afraid of those who kill the body and after that can do no more. 5But I will show you whom you should fear: Fear the*

One who, after you have been killed, has authority to throw you into hell. Yes, I tell you, fear Him! It is a snare (trap) to do wrong so that you can win favor with mankind.

Proverbs 30

The Sayings of Agur

1 The words of Agur the son of Jakeh, the oracle.
  The man declares to Ithiel,
  to Ithiel and Ukal:

2 Surely I am more brutish than any man,
  and have not the understanding of a man.

3 I neither learned wisdom,
  nor have the knowledge of the holy.

4 Who has ascended up into heaven, or descended?
  Who has gathered the wind in his fists?
  Who has bound the waters in a garment?
  Who has established all the ends of the earth?
  What is His name, and what is the name of His son,
  if you know?

5 Every word of God is pure;
  He is a shield to those who put their trust in Him.

6 Do not add to His words,
  lest He reprove you, and you be found a liar.

7 Two things I have required of you;
  do not deny me them before I die:

8 Remove vanity and lies far from me—

give me neither poverty nor riches;
    feed me with food convenient for me;

9 lest I be full, and deny You,
    and say, "Who is the Lord?"
    or lest I be poor, and steal,
    and take the name of my God in vain.

10 Do not accuse a servant to his master,
    lest he curse you, and you be found guilty.

11 There is a generation that curses their father,
    and does not bless its mother.

12 There is a generation that is pure in its own eyes,
    and yet is not washed from its filthiness.

13 There is a generation—oh, how lofty are their eyes!
    And their eyelids are lifted up.

14 There is a generation whose teeth are as swords,
    and their jaw teeth as knives,
    to devour the poor from off the earth,
    and the needy from among men.

15 The leech has two daughters,
    crying, "Give, give."

    There are three things that are never satisfied,
    indeed, four things never say, "It is enough":

16 the grave, the barren womb,
    the earth that is not filled with water,
    and the fire that never says, "It is enough."

17 The eye that mocks at his father,

and despises to obey his mother,
the ravens of the valley will pick it out,
and the young eagles will eat it.

18 There are three things which are too wonderful for me,
indeed, four which I do not know:

19 the way of an eagle in the air,
the way of a serpent on a rock,
the way of a ship in the midst of the sea,
and the way of a man with a maid.

20 Such is the way of an adulterous woman;
she eats and wipes her mouth,
and says, "I have done no wickedness."

21 For three things the earth is disquieted,
and for four which it cannot bear:

22 for a servant when he reigns,
and a fool when he is filled with food,
23 for a hateful woman when she is married,

and a handmaid who is heir to her mistress.

24 There are four things which are little upon the earth,
but they are exceeding wise:

25 The ants are a people not strong,
yet they prepare their food in the summer;

26 the badgers are but a feeble folk,
yet they make their houses in the rocks;

27 the locusts have no king,
yet they go forth all of them by bands;

28 the spider takes hold with her hands,
   and is in kings' palaces.

29 There are three things which go well,
   indeed, four are comely in going:

30 a lion which is strongest among beasts,
   and does not turn away for any;

31 a strutting rooster, a male goat also,
   and a king, against whom there is no rising up.

32 If you have been foolish in lifting up yourself,
   or if you have thought evil,
   put your hand on your mouth.

33 Surely the churning of milk brings forth butter,
   and the wringing of the nose brings forth blood,
   so the forcing of wrath brings forth strife.

Note:

verse 25 *The ants are a people not strong, yet they prepare their food in the summer*

Proverbs 30:25 might be my favorite verse in the entire book of Proverbs. I call the teaching 'ant wise'. It reminds me that 'big shovel fulls is not the only way to move sand'. You might not be the biggest or strongest person, but that does not mean that work can not get done. Its like what a former teacher once told me 'an elephant is ate with one bite at a time'. So use your head and think of ways to multiply the work that you do.

Proverbs 31

The Sayings of King Lemuel's Mother

1 The words of King Lemuel, an oracle that his mother taught him:

2 What, my son? And what, the son of my womb?
  And what, the son of my vows?

3 Do not give your strength to women,
  nor your ways to that which destroys kings.

4 It is not for kings, O Lemuel,
  it is not for kings to drink wine,
  nor for princes strong drink;

5 lest they drink and forget the law,
  and pervert the justice of any of the afflicted.

6 Give strong drink to him who is ready to perish,
  and wine to those who are of heavy hearts.

7 Let him drink, and forget his poverty,
  and remember his misery no more.

8 Open your mouth for the speechless
  in the cause of all such as are appointed to destruction.

9 Open your mouth, judge righteously,
  and plead the cause of the poor and needy.

Epilogue: The Virtuous Wife

10 Who can find a virtuous woman?
  For her worth is far above rubies.

11 The heart of her husband safely trusts in her,
  so that he will have no lack of gain.

12 She will do him good and not evil
   all the days of her life.

13 She seeks wool and flax,
   and works willingly with her hands.

14 She is like the merchant ships,
   she brings her food from afar.

15 She also rises while it is yet night,
   and gives food to her household,
   and a portion to her maidens.

16 She considers a field and buys it;
   with the fruit of her hands she plants a vineyard.

17 She clothes herself with strength,
   and strengthens her arms.

18 She perceives that her merchandise is good;
   her candle does not go out by night.

19 She lays her hands to the spindle,
   and her hands hold the distaff.

20 She stretches out her hand to the poor;
   yes, she reaches forth her hands to the needy.

21 She is not afraid of the snow for her household,
   for all her household are clothed with scarlet.

22 She makes herself coverings of tapestry;
   her clothing is silk and purple.

23 Her husband is known in the gates,
   when he sits among the elders of the land.

24 She makes fine linen and sells it,
   and delivers sashes to the merchant.

25 Strength and honor are her clothing,
   and she will rejoice in time to come.

26 She opens her mouth with wisdom,
   and in her tongue is the teaching of kindness.

27 She looks well to the ways of her household,
   and does not eat the bread of idleness.

28 Her children rise up and call her blessed;
   her husband also, and he praises her:

29 "Many daughters have done virtuously,
   but you excel them all."

30 Charm is deceitful, and beauty is vain,
   but a woman who fears the Lord, she shall be praised.

31 Give her of the fruit of her hands,
   and let her own works praise her in the gates.

Note:

Proverbs 31:10-31 Statistics say that almost 50 percent of all marriages in the United States will end in divorce or separation. That means that a person can get airplane and jump out of the window and the first person that they land on, those two people can get married. That airplane marriage has about as much of a chance of working as someone that spends 2 years getting to know someone. So it is obvious that Proverbs 31:10-31 is welcomed marriage advice. I personally think that if the only thing that a couple has going for them is that 'they are in love' then its probably a bad idea to get married. Remember that back in Genesis 1:28 GOD told mankind that they had a job to do. I know that it is tempting but instead of scoring people based on the size of there bank account...or the size of other part of them why don't we try to start scoring people based on there ability to help us do the job that GOD gave us! Why not try to marry someone that can help us do what GOD told us to do? I think that more people need to work on being more virtuous, and at the same time more people need to start seeing the value of someone that is trying to live virtuous lifestyle.

(Any Bible passage can be found by going to www.biblehub.com and to further examine any Bible verse click on the 'comment' tab!)

Final Thoughts

A number of years ago I was told that if I was to read one chapter in the Book of Proverbs every day then in most months I would read through the entire book of Proverbs. I think that such a reading plan is a good idea, however after becoming familiar with the book I would encourage readers to follow the following reading plan:

- On the first day of the month, read the first verse in the chapter and allow the words to penetrate you.

- On the second day of the month, read the first two verses in the chapter and meditate on the words.

- On the third day of the month, read the first three verses in the chapter and hold fast to the words.

- And so on and so on.

How many people do you know that can honestly say that they have mastered every lesson that this life has to teach them? I imagine that it is about the same number of people that can benefit from reading the book of Proverbs only once.

Sometimes I think about how to teach everybody. Of course I am not smart enough to do that but fortunately GOD is an absolute genius and HE wrote a book that can teach everyone. So I will recommend the book that HE has written. The books that GOD wrote can be used to instruct children, teach youth, advise young adults, guide seasoned adults, reform detainees, and rehabilitate those battling addictions...and a book that is useful for all sorts of ages and all sorts of situations is the book of Proverbs.

Ecclesiastics Introduction

Previously we read how JESUS has said that mammon (and not some ambiguous devil) is the enemy of The Kingdom of GOD. In any conflict the targets need to be identified. Your not going to win unless you first know who your fighting. And satan is a pawn in the hands of the LORD. I am tired of people thinking that they are locked in a battle with the devil, let me say that some people are locked in a battle with themselves. They think that the tempter is outside the gate, but sometimes I think that there are more devils sitting in church than what hells got! If people would like a clear picture of who is tempting them then they should look in the mirror.

James 1:14-15

> 14 _Temptation comes from our own desires_, which entice us and drag us away. 15 These desires give birth to sinful actions. And when sin is allowed to grow, it gives birth to death.

Like I said, I want this book to be like a road sign that informs people of how they should act (because the church aint doing it). JESUS pointed out that HE has a Kingdom, and the rogue kingdom is headed by mammon. In Genesis when sin entered the world, that was the first attempted coup on earth (because 'sin' is rebellion against the KING). Churches want to twist the WORD and confuse people but 'to sin' is an old archery term that means to miss the mark (or target). The target is to live like the KING instructed. In Matthew 11:30 JESUS said that HIS yoke is easy and HIS burden is light... so if you have missed the target and shot a bird, what you have done is not an unintentional action. Serving mammon just means not following the teachings of the KING. So it really does not matter who or what you think that you are serving, because if you are not living your life the way that the KING has ordered then you are serving mammon.

Matthew 6:24

> **No one can serve two masters; for either he will hate the one and love the other, or else he will be loyal to the one and despise the other. You cannot serve God and mammon.**

Is anyone else amazed by how smart people think that they are? The only way that mammon is able to gather up a following is because people are so easily duped. There is a Chinese proverb that says 'the fool tests the depth of the water with both feet', but the man that tests the debts of the water with both feet is certain that he has a good idea. I am trying to point out that sometimes people do not question the intelligence of there plans until it might be to late.

I enjoy seeing the irony in various situations, and a piece of irony that is pointed out in the Biblical book of Ecclesiastics is that some people work, work, work there whole lives. I am not talking about working to put food on the table, or working to provide for their families. I am talking about those people that work there lives away and miss out on their kids growing up because they are busy chasing the 'almighty dollar', and then one day they die and they have to give all of there money to someone else. When a person is young they trade their time for other people's money, and when those people get older they try to trade their money for just a little more time.

The Book of Ecclesiastics is probably my favorite Book of the Bible because it allows me the opportunity to learn from other people's mistakes. There are two ways to learn things: #1 You can learn things the hard way (which sometimes involves personal pain), or #2 You can learn the easy way (which sometimes means watching other people make mistakes), and Ecclesiastics saves me a lot of time and effort by inviting me to look at a misguided life.

As you are reading through the book, there are 5 points to keep in mind:

1. **You are not going to leave this life with any material positions.**

"As he came forth of his mother's womb, naked shall he return to go as he came, and shall take nothing of his labor, which he may carry away in his hand". **Ecclesiastes 5:15**

2. **We all need to be aware of the times that we are living in.**

"To everything, there is a season and a time to every purpose under the heaven." Ecclesiastes 3:1. GOD did not create the whole world in one day instead GOD prioritized HIS work...we also need to prioritize things!

3. **You cant get on your horse and ride off in all directions.**

"Whatsoever thy hand findeth to do, do it with thy might; for there is no work, nor device, nor knowledge, nor wisdom, in the grave, whither thou goest." Ecclesiastes 9:10. There are 101 different jobs that you can do during the day and one of the jobs is that you can move a pile of sand with a pair of tweezers...but why would you want to do that. Think before you act...fulfillment is found only when God is involved.

4. **Remember that life is short and eternity is a long time.**

Remember your Creator in the days of your youth, before the difficult days come and the years arrive when you say, "I have no pleasure in them" Ecclesiastes 12:1 GOD wants people to enjoy our existence, just remember that how we conduct ourselves while we are on this earth is going to echo for eternity.

5. **Lets weigh the matter.**

When all has been heard, the conclusion of the matter is this: Fear God and keep HIS commandments, because this is the whole duty of man. Ecclesiastes 12:13 A fool will gladly exchange an unknown amount of riches for a shiny penny, so is the person that fights tooth and nail for a prestigious position here on earth.

The Book of Ecclesiastes

Chapter 1

1 These are the words of the teacher (Hebrew, *Qoheleth,* one who gathers), the son of David, king in Jerusalem.

2 **Teacher:** Life is fleeting, like a passing mist. *It is like trying to catch hold of a breath;* All vanishes like a vapor; everything is a great vanity. 3 What good does it do anyone to work so hard *again and again,* sun up to sundown? *All his labor to gain but a little?* 4 One generation comes, another goes; but the earth continues to remain. 5 The sun rises and the sun sets, laboring to come up quickly to its place again *and again.* 6 The wind in its travels blows toward the south, then swings back around to the north. Back and forth, returning in its circuit again *and again.* 7 All rivers flow to the sea, but the sea is never full. To the place where the rivers flow, there the water returns to flow once again. 8 Words, words, words! So many words! They are wearisome things; and yet people cannot refrain from speaking. No eye has ever surveyed *the world* and said, "I have seen enough"; no ear has ever listened *to creation* and said, "I have heard enough." 9 What has been, that will be; what has been done, that will be done. Nothing is new under the sun; *the future only repeats the past.* 10 One person may say of some idea, "Pay attention to this; it's original!" But that same idea has already been expressed; it's been with us through the ages.

11 We do not remember those people *and events* of long ago, as future generations will not remember what is yet to come.

12 I, the teacher, was king over Israel in Jerusalem. 13 I decided to seek out and study the wisdom *of the ages,* of all that had been done under the heavens. *I soon discovered* the harsh realities of the work God has given us that keeps us so busy. 14 I have witnessed all that is done under the sun, and indeed, all is fleeting, like trying to embrace the wind. 15 *There is an old saying:*

> 'Something crooked cannot be made straight, and something missing cannot be counted.'

16 I *mused over it all and* thought to myself, "I have done great things, and I have gained more wisdom than anyone who reigned over Jerusalem before me. I have contemplated great wisdom and knowledge." 17 I decided to study wisdom and *instead acquainted myself with* madness and folly. It, too, seemed like trying to pursue the wind, 18 for as *my* wisdom increased, so did *my* vexation. As *my* knowledge grew, so did *my* pain.

Chapter 2

1 **Teacher:** I said to myself, "Let me dabble and test you in pleasure and see if there is any good *in that.*" But look, that, too, was fleeting. 2 Of laughter I said, "Foolishness." Of pleasure, "And in the end what is accomplished?" 3 So I thought about drinking wine, for it soothes the flesh. But all the while my mind was filled with thoughts of wisdom—about how to rein in foolishness—until I might understand the best way for us to live out our brief lives and number of days under heaven. 4 *Next,* I began some enormous projects, building my own houses and planting my own vineyards. 5 I designed *impressive* gardens and parks and planted them with all kinds of

fruit trees. 6 I installed pools of water to irrigate the forests of young saplings. 7 I acquired male and female servants; I even had servants born into my household. I had herds *of cattle,* flocks *of sheep and goats*—more than anyone who had ever lived in Jerusalem before me. 8 I amassed a fortune in silver and gold, and *I stockpiled* the treasures of kings and provinces. I hired men and women to sing *and entertain me,* and *I pampered myself with* what every man desires—many women. 9 I *surrounded myself with all this and* became great, far greater than anyone who had ever lived in Jerusalem before me. And still, my wisdom never left my side. 10 *Throughout this experiment,* I let myself have anything my eyes desired, and I did not withhold from my mind any pleasure. *What was the conclusion?* My mind found joy in all the work I did—my work was its own reward! 11 As I continued musing over all I had accomplished and the hard work it took, *I concluded that* all this, too, was fleeting, like trying to embrace the wind. Is there any real gain *by all our hard work* under the sun?

12 I turned my attention to *the ways of* wisdom and folly and madness. *I asked,* "What is left for those who come after the king to do? They can only repeat what he has already done." 13 I realized that wisdom is better than folly, just as light is better than darkness. 14 *As the old saying goes:*

> 'The wise have eyes in their heads, but fools stumble in the darkness.'

Yet I knew *deep down* that the same fate comes to both of them. 15 I said to myself, "Why do I try to be wise when my fate is the same as that of the fool? This pursuit is fleeting too." 16 Neither the wise nor the fool will be remembered for very long *once they are gone.* The wise dies, and the fool alike. All are forgotten in the future. 17 So I began to hate life itself because all that is done under the sun is so harsh and difficult. Life—everything about it—is fleeting; it's like trying to pursue the wind.

18 So I began to hate all the hard work I had done under the sun because I would *eventually* have to leave it all to the one who comes after me. 19 And who knows whether my heir will be wise or foolish? Still he will inherit all the things for which I worked so hard here under the sun, the things for which I became wise. This, too, is fleeting *like trying to catch hold of a breath*. 20 So I turned these thoughts over in my mind and despaired over how hard I worked under the sun. 21 Although someone with wisdom, knowledge, and skill works hard, *when he departs this life,* he will leave all he has accomplished to another who has done nothing to deserve work's reward. This, too, is fleeting, and *it causes* great misery. 22 What exactly do people get out of all their work and all the stresses they put themselves through here under the sun? 23 For every day is filled with pain and every job has its own problems, and there are nights when the mind doesn't stop and rest. And once again, this is fleeting. 24 There is nothing better than for people to eat and drink and to see the good in their hard work. These *beautiful gifts,* I realized, too, come from God's hand. 25 For who can eat and *drink and* enjoy *the good things* if not me? 26 To those who *seek to* please God, He gives wisdom and knowledge and joyfulness; but to those who are wicked, God keeps them busy harvesting and storing up for those in whom He delights. But even this is fleeting; it's like trying to embrace the wind.

Chapter 3

1 **Teacher:** For everything *that happens in life*—there is a season, a right time for everything under heaven:

2 A time to be born, a time to die;
a time to plant, a time to collect the harvest;

3 A time to kill, a time to heal;
a time to tear down, a time to build up;
4 A time to cry, a time to laugh;
a time to mourn, a time to dance;
5 A time to scatter stones, a time to pile them up;
a time for a *warm* embrace, a time for keeping your distance;
6 A time to search, a time to give up as lost;
a time to keep, a time to throw out;
7 A time to tear apart, a time to bind together;
a time to be quiet, a time to speak up;
8 A time to love, a time to hate;
a time to go to war, a time to make peace.

9 What good comes to anyone who works so hard, all to gain *a few possessions?* 10 I have seen the *kinds of* tasks God has given each of us to do to keep one busy, 11 *and I know* God has made everything beautiful for its time. God has also placed in our minds a sense of eternity; we look back on the past and ponder over the future, yet we cannot understand the doings of God. 12 I know there is nothing better for us than to be joyful and to do good throughout our lives; 13 to eat and drink and see the good in all of our hard work is a gift from God. 14 I know everything God does endures for all time. Nothing can be added to it; nothing can be taken away from it. We humans can only stand in awe of all God has done. 15 What has been and what is to be—already is. And God holds accountable all the pursuits of humanity.

--(side note) The contrast between God and humanity could not be starker. The teacher drives this point home by reminding his reader that human lives and earthly accomplishments are fleeting. Nothing tangible is permanent. No work lasts. It all slips away and vanishes into thin air. Compare that to God. Everything God does is substantial. Everything God accomplishes lasts forever. Every word God speaks makes a difference. And so, God places within every person a sense of eternity to know (the fact that life is temporary) yet not understand Him. (So I can understand why some people are depressed...they are believing the lies of society that say that there is no GOD, but they are smart enough to figure out that 'any physical asset is temporary'. So they are like a camel trying to go through a doggie door and they are asking themselves 'What is going on?') This world with all its goodness and beauty is not as good as it gets. There is more, so much more, and we are made for that reality too. But not now, not yet. (end side note)--

Teacher: 16 Again, I looked *at everything that goes on* under the sun and realized that in place of justice, wickedness prevails. In place of righteousness, wrongdoing succeeds. 17 I said to myself, "God will judge the righteous and the wicked, for there is a right time for every pursuit and for every action." 18 I thought about how people act: "God *often* puts them to the test to show them how much they are like the animals." 19 The fate of humans and the fate of animals is the same. As one dies, so does the other, for we have the same breath within us. *In the end,* we have no advantage over the animals. For *as I have said,* it's all fleeting. 20 Humans and animals alike go to one place; all are *formed* from dust, and all return to the dust *once more.* 21 Who really knows whether the spirits of human beings go up and the spirits of animals go down into the earth? 22 So I realized there is nothing better for us than to find joy in the work we do, for work is its own reward. For who will bring us back to see what will be after we are gone?

Chapter 4

1 **Teacher:** Then I looked again and saw all the oppression that happens under the sun. I saw the tears of the oppressed, and no one

offered to *help and* comfort them. The oppressors exercise *all* the power, while the powerless have no one to *help and* comfort them. 2 It struck me that the dead are actually better off than the living who must go on living; 3 and, even better, are those who were never born in the first place. At least they have never had to witness all of the injustices that take place under the sun.

--(Side note)The imbalance of power creates many victims. Worldly power, sourced in corrupt systems "under the sun," is on the side of the oppressor. (As has been discussed, The Kingdom of GOD is opposed by the kingdom of mammon, and take a guess at which kingdom is selfish.) Few are in the ditches with the broken and poor.(But hopefully this book will persuade a few more people that the purpose of this life is to oppose the kingdom of mammon) (End side note)--

Teacher: 4 Then I saw *yet another thing*: *envy fuels achievement.* All the work and skills people develop come from their desire to be better than their neighbors. Even this is fleeting, like trying to embrace the wind.

--(Side note)(Verse 4 was a clear cut definition of why capitalism works...people are not designed for communism/socialism to work) (End note)--

5 *As the saying goes*:

> 'The fool folds his hands *to rest* and lets his flesh waste away.'

6 And it is better to have one handful of peace than to have two hands full of hard work and a desire to catch the wind.

7 Again I observed *another example of* how fleeting life is under the sun: 8 a person who is all alone—with no child, no sibling—yet he

works hard his entire life. Still he is never satisfied with the wealth he gains. Does he stop to ask, "Why am I working so hard?" or "Why am I depriving myself of life's *simple* pleasures?" This, too, is fleeting, *like trying to catch hold of a breath;* it's a miserable situation.

9 Two are better than one because a good return comes when two work *together.* 10 If one of them falls, the other can help him up. But who will help the pitiful person who falls down alone? 11 In the same way, if two lie down together, they can keep each other warm. But how will the one who sleeps alone stay warm *against the night*? 12 And if one person is vulnerable to attack, two can drive the attacker away. *As the saying goes,* "A rope made of three strands is not quickly broken."

13 A poor, wise youth is better off than an old, foolish king who no longer accepts advice. 14 *For example,* once a young man marched out of prison to become king; it had not mattered how poor he once had been in his kingdom. 15 I saw all those who live out their lives under the sun flock to the side of a second youth who took the king's place. 16 There seemed to be no limit to all the people who were under his authority. Yet those who will come later will not be happy with him *and will refuse to follow him*. Even this, you see, is fleeting—*power and influence do not last*—like trying to pursue the wind.

Chapter 5

1 **Teacher:** Watch your step when you enter the house of God. Be ready to listen *quietly* rather than *rushing in* to offer up a sacrifice to foolish people, for they have no idea that what they do is evil.

God knows what is on the inside. Words and actions are not always necessary.

2 Do not be too hasty to speak your mind before God or too quick to

make promises *you won't keep,* for God is in heaven and you are on earth. Therefore, *watch your tongue;* let your words be few. 3 For just as busyness breeds *restless* dreams, so wordiness reveals the voice of a fool.

4 If you make a promise to God, do not be slow to keep it; for He takes no pleasure in fools. So do what you have promised. 5 *In fact,* it would be better not to make a vow *in the first place* than to make it and not fulfill it. 6 Do not let your mouth lead you to sin, and do not claim before the temple messenger that your vow was a mistake. Why should God be angry at the sound of your voice and destroy everything you've worked hard to achieve? 7 Daydreaming and excessive talking are pointless *and fleeting things to do, like trying to catch hold of a breath. What good comes from them? It is better to* quietly reverence God.

8 If you see the poor oppressed, justice denied, and righteousness rejected in a particular place, then do not be surprised at this; for those in power are watched over by those higher up, and they *in turn* by some even higher. 9 *Still,* it is better for the land *in every way* to have a king who cultivates the fields.

Corruption often starts at the top and works its way down.

10 *As the saying goes:*

> 'Those who love money will never be satisfied with
> money, and those who love riches will never be happy
> with what they have.'

This, too, is fleeting. 11 The more goods there are, the more people there are to consume them. How does any of this really benefit the owners except they can gaze *proudly* on their possessions? 12 Sweet sleep comes to those who work hard, regardless of how much or how little they've eaten. But the abundance of the rich keeps them awake *at night*.

--(Side note)There is nothing like the sense of gratification that comes from working hard all day, when bread and cheese taste as good as the finest steak. The ability to work, strength to work, and desire for work are all gifts from God. When we understand that and use the gifts that GOD has given us accordingly, simple things like sleep and a good meal are causes for joy and celebration. But those who are rich and idle can't buy a good night's sleep or a stress-free meal or a moment's peace. (End note)--

Teacher: 13 I have witnessed a grave evil *pervading our world,* one that has been with us since the first sunrise: harm comes to all who hoard their riches. 14 Such riches can easily vanish through some misfortune, so that the rich have nothing left to pass along to their children. 15 We all came naked from our mother's womb, and we will leave this world as we came, taking nothing of the wealth for which we have toiled. 16 Here, too, is another grave evil: all of us, *no matter who we are,* will depart this world exactly the same way as we came into it. So what good does it do to continue to toil after the wind? 17 So all our days we eat in darkness, with mounting frustration, suffering, and anger.

18 Then it dawned on me that this is good and proper: to eat and drink and find the good in all the toil that we undertake under the sun during the few days God has given, for this is our lot *in life.* 19 Also, God gives wealth, possessions, and power to enjoy those things, and He allows them to accept their lot *in life* and to enjoy hard work. This is God's gift. 20 For people like this have no time to despair over life because God keeps them so busy with a deep-seated joy.

Chapter 6

1 **Teacher:** I have seen another injustice under the sun, one that is a real burden upon humanity. 2 *Sometimes* God gives money, possessions, and even honor, so that we have everything a person might desire; nothing is lacking. But then, *for reasons God only knows,* God does not allow him to enjoy the good gifts. Rather, a stranger ends up enjoying them. This, too, is fleeting; it's a sickening evil. 3 If a person has one hundred children and lives for many years but finds no satisfaction in all of the good things *that life brings* and *in the end* doesn't have a proper burial, I say that it would be better if that person had been stillborn 4 because the stillborn arrives in a fleeting breath and then goes nameless into the darkness *mourned by no one and buried in an unmarked grave.* 5 Though the child never sees the sun or knows anything, it still had more rest than the person *who cannot enjoy what he has.* 6 Even if a person were to live one thousand years twice over, but could find no satisfaction, don't we all end up going to the same place? (That is we all end up in the grave)

--(Side note) The words, "it would be better if that person had been stillborn," may shock the modern reader because it is hoped that no child is stillborn; believers pray for a good life for all of God's creatures. But the writer of Ecclesiastes does not dwell on the fate of the stillborn; instead he contrasts the life of the person who finds no good in life with the fate of the child who never drew breath, never saw the sun, and never was given a name. Life is a gift from God, and the teacher admonishes his readers to find the good in that gift. Yes, sometimes life is not fair; yes, sometimes life deals harsh blows; yes, life slips away far too quickly. But as long as someone draws breath, he or she should find the good in that life.(End note)--

Teacher: 7 *As the saying goes,* "All of our toil is food for our mouths." *We eat; we drink,* and yet deep down we do not feel satisfied. 8 What good is it to be wise? Are the wise better off than fools? And what do the poor know that others do not when they conduct themselves before the public? 9 It is better to enjoy what our eyes see than to long for what our *roving* appetites desire. This, too, is fleeting, like trying to embrace the wind.

10 Whatever exists has already been named. Human nature, as it is *with its strengths and limitations*, is already known. So no one dares to dispute with One so much stronger than he. 11 The more a person speaks, the more breath is fleeting; and what advantage do a lot of words bring us? 12 For who knows the best way for us to live during the few days of our fleeting lives? *After all,* we pass through them like shadows. For who can say what will happen under the sun after we are gone?

Chapter 7

1 **Teacher:** A good name is worth more than the finest perfume, and the day you die is better than the day you were born.

2 *In the same way,* it is better to go to a funeral than a celebration. *Why?* because death is the end of life's journey, and the living should always take that to heart.

3 Sorrow beats *foolish* laughter; embracing sadness somehow gladdens our hearts.

4 A wise heart is well acquainted with grief, but a foolish heart seeks only pleasure's company.

5 It is better to hear the rebuke of the wise than a song written by fools,

6 For the laughter of fools is like the *hiss and* crackle of burning thorns beneath a pot. This, too, is fleeting.

7 Oppression *can* turn the wise into fools, and a bribe *can* damage the *noblest* heart.

8 Having the last word is better than having the first, and patience *will benefit you* more than pride.

9 Do not be quick to anger, for anger sits *comfortably* in the lap of fools.

10 Do not ask, "Where have all the good times gone?" Wisdom knows better than to ask such a thing.

11 It is good to have wisdom along with an inheritance; *they give* a *clear* advantage to those who see the sun.

12 For *together* wisdom and money are alike in this: both offer protection *from life's misfortunes,*
But the *real* advantage of knowledge is this: wisdom *alone* preserves the lives of those who have it.

13 Think *for a moment* about the work of God. Can anyone make straight what God has made crooked?

14 When times are good, *enjoy them and* be happy. When times are bad, think about this: God makes both *good and bad times,* so that no one really knows what is coming next.

15 In the fleeting time I have lived on this earth, I have seen *just about* everything: the good dying in their goodness and the wicked living to a ripe old age. 16 *So my advice?* Do not act overly righteous, and do not *think yourself* wiser than others. Why *go and* ruin yourself? 17 But do not be too wicked or foolish either. Why die before it's your time? 18 Grasp both sides of things and keep the two in balance; for anyone who fears God won't give in to the extremes.

– (Side note) When Cain is distressed over God's choice of Abel's offering over his, God says to Cain, *"Don't you know that* as long as you do what is right, then I accept you? But if you do not do what is right, *watch out, because* sin is crouching at the door, ready to pounce on you!" Genesis 4:7. The temptation to scheme—that is, to do the "evil" rather than the "good"—begins with the first human pair; the teacher of Ecclesiastes reminds his readers that the same temptation still exists. (End note) --

19 Wisdom is more powerful to a wise person than 10 rulers in a city.

20 There is not a righteous person on earth who *always* does good and never sins.

21 Don't take to heart all that people say; *eventually* you may hear your servant curse you.

22 And face it, your heart has overheard how often you've cursed others.

23 I have tested all of these sayings against wisdom. I promised myself, "I will become wise," but wisdom kept its distance.

24 *True* wisdom *remains elusive*; its profound mysteries are remote. Who can discover it?

25 So I *turned and* dedicated my heart to knowing *more,* to digging *deeper,* to searching *harder* for wisdom and the reasons things are as they are. I applied myself to understanding the connection between wickedness and folly, between folly and madness.

26 *Along this journey,* I discovered something more bitter than death—a seductive woman. Her heart is a trap and net. Her hands shackle *your wrists.* Those who seek to please God will escape her clutches, but sinners will be caught in her trap.

27 Look at this! After investigating the matter thoroughly to find out why things are as they are,

28 I realize that although I kept on searching, I have not found *what I am looking for*. Only one man in a thousand have I found, but I could not find a single woman among all of these *who knows this*.

29 Here is what I have figured out: God made humanity for good, but *we* humans go out and scheme our way *into trouble*.

Chapter 8

1 **Teacher:**

How rare to find one who is truly wise, one who knows how to interpret this *or solve that*!

Wisdom brightens the countenance of the face, and softens hard lines *etched* in the face.

2 Here's my advice: keep what comes from the king's mouth; after all, this matter is really an oath from God. 3 Don't be in a hurry to leave the king's presence or throw your support behind a bad cause, because the king can do whatever he wishes. 4 Since the king has the power to enforce his word, who dares ask him, "What are you doing?" 5 Whoever does what the king commands will stay out of trouble, and the wise heart will figure out the proper time and proper way *to proceed*. 6 Yes, there is a time and a way to deal with every situation, even when a person's troubles are on the rise. 7 For no one knows what is going to happen, so who can warn him before it does? 8 No one can master the wind and contain it—*it blows as it will*. No one has power over the day of death—*it comes as it will*. No soldier is discharged in *the heat of* battle, and certainly wickedness will not

release those entangled in it. 9 I have witnessed all of this as I have focused my attention on all that is done under the sun: whenever one person oppresses another to lift himself up, it only hurts him *in the end.*

10 I have witnessed the wicked buried *with honor* because during their lifetimes they would go in and out of the temple, and soon their *crimes* were forgotten in the very city where they committed them. This, too, is fleeting. 11 When the penalty for a crime is not carried out quickly, then people start scheming to commit their own crimes. 12 Although a wicked person commits a hundred sins and still lives a long life, I am confident it will go better for those who worship the one True God and stand in awe before Him, 13 and it will not go well for the wicked nor will their days grow long like *evening* shadows because they do not stand in awe of God.

14 Here is another example of the fleeting nature of our world: there are just people who get what the wicked deserve; there are wicked people who get what the just deserve. I say this, too, is fleeting. 15 And so I *heartily* recommended *that you pursue* joy, for the best a person can do under the sun is to *enjoy life.* Eat, drink, and be happy. *If this is your attitude,* joy will carry you through the toil every day that God gives you under the sun.

16 When I applied myself to the study of wisdom and reflected on the *kinds of* tasks that occupy people's attention on earth, I noticed how little sleep they generally get, whether day or night. 17 I saw all the works *and ways* of God, and it became clear to me that no one is able to grasp fully this *mystery called life.* Try as we might, we cannot discover what has been done under the sun. Even if the wise claim to know, they really haven't discovered it.

Chapter 9

1 **Teacher:** So I set my mind on all of this, examined it thoroughly, and *here's what I think:* The righteous and the wise and *all* their deeds are in God's hands. Whether they are *destined to be* loved or hated, no one *but God* knows. 2 Everyone shares a common destiny—the righteous and the wicked, the good [and the bad], the clean and the unclean, those who sacrifice and those who neglect the sacrifices. The good *and the faithful* are treated no differently than the sinner. Those who take an oath are treated no differently than those afraid to commit. *Such a great injustice!* 3 Here is an evil that pervades all that is done under the sun: the same destiny happens to us all. Human hearts are inclined toward evil; madness runs deep throughout our lives. And then what happens? We die. 4 So long as we are alive, we have hope; it is better to be a living dog, *you see,* than a dead lion. 5 At least the living know they will die; the dead don't know anything. *No future,* no reward is awaiting them, and one day they will be completely forgotten. 6 All of their love and hate and envy die with them; then it is too late to share in the *human* struggle under the sun.

--(Side note) At best, life is unpredictable. No one knows whether a pleasant or harsh future awaits. Perhaps it is better that way. It would be nice if good actions always guaranteed a pleasant future, but they don't. Sometimes, in this fallen world (i.e. the kingdom of mammon), it is just the opposite. One thing is certain, however: everyone faces death. It is the great equalizer. Yet the teacher is assured of something else: those who are right with God and live wisely are in His hands. (End note) --

Teacher: 7 So *here is what you should do:* go and enjoy your meals, drink your wine and love *every minute of* it because God is already pleased with what you do. 8 Dress your best, and don't forget a splash of scented fragrance. 9 Enjoy life with the woman you love. Cherish every moment of the fleeting life which God has given you under the sun. For this is your lot in life, *your great reward* for all of your hard work under the sun. 10 Whatever you find to do, do it well because where you are going—the grave—there will be no working or thinking or knowing or wisdom.

11 I turned and witnessed *something else* under the sun: the race does not *always* go to the swift, the battle is not *always* won by the strong, bread does not *always* fill *the table of* the wise, wealth does not *always* accrue to the skillful, and favor is not *always* granted to the knowledgeable; but time and misfortune happen to them all. 12 A person can't possibly know when his time will come. Like fish caught in a cruel net or birds trapped in a snare, without warning the unexpected happens, and people are caught up in an evil time.

When tragedy strikes, neither our wisdom nor our wealth nor our power can spare us from it.

13 I have witnessed an example of wisdom under the sun and admit I found it impressive: 14 Once there was a small town with only a few people in it. One day, *out of nowhere,* a king *and his* powerful *army* marched against it, surrounded it, and besieged it. *The villagers didn't know how to fend off such a powerful enemy.* 15 But one man, who was *very* poor but *very* wise, *rallied the villagers and managed to drive the army away.* (*The village remains to this day,* but no one remembers the name of that one wise man who saved the village.) 16 So I said, "Wisdom is better than strength." But the wisdom of the poor is despised; nobody listens to their *wise* counsel.

17 It is better to hear the soft-spoken words of a wise person than the rant of a tyrant in the company of fools.

18 Wisdom is better than weapons of war, yet one wrongdoer can undo much good.

Chapter 10

1 **Teacher:** *Remember the saying,*

> 'Dead flies can spoil a good perfume.'

In the same way, all the wisdom and honor *in the world* cannot out-weigh a moment's folly.
2 Wise people move to the right *where they honor the goodness of God's creation,*
while fools move to the left *and choose to ignore it.*

--(Side note) Verse two states that "wise people move to the right.... while fools move to the left." The contrast between "right" and "left" reflects the ancient Near Eastern ideas of "clean" and "unclean." The right hand was considered the clean hand and was a symbol for pros-perity, while the left hand was considered the unclean hand and a symbol for disaster. The clean hand was used for eating, for acts of hospitality, and for greeting others. The unclean hand was used for personal hygiene. Thus, in this metaphor the right is equated with God's goodness, while the left is equated with ignorance of God's goodness. (End note)--

3 **Teacher:** Fools are easily spotted when they walk down the street: their lack of sense is obvious to everyone.
4 If someone in charge becomes angry at you, don't leave your post; a calm reply puts great offenses to rest.

5 I have seen another *restless* evil in this world, the kind of error that arises from those in power: 6 *fools and their* folly are promoted to positions of authority, while the rich *and talented* are assigned menial tasks. 7 I have seen slaves riding on horseback *like royalty* and princes walking on the ground like slaves.

8 If you dig a pit, you may fall into it. If you tear down an old wall, a

snake may come out and bite you.

9 Whoever quarries stones may be crushed by them, and whoever splits wood may be hurt *by flying debris*.

10 If a tool is dull and no one sharpens its edge, the work will be harder; the advantage of wisdom is *this: it brings* success.

11 If a snake bites before it is charmed, there is no advantage in being a *snake* charmer.

12 The words of the wise bring them favor, but those of the foolish endanger them.

13 The first words out of a fool's mouth are folly; the last words he utters are evil madness.

14 The fool babbles on and on, *not knowing when to stop.* Though no one knows what will happen next, *he may think he knows.* Who can tell what the future holds?

15 The fools' work wears them out; *they're so weary* they can't find their way to the city.

16 Woe to the land whose king is a child and whose princes start their feast in the morning.

17 Blessed is the land whose king is of noble heritage and whose princes know when to feast, *Who discipline themselves* with strength and avoid drunkenness.

18 The roof sags over the head of lazybones; the house leaks because of idle hands.

19 Feasts are happy occasions; wine brings joy to life; money is the answer for everything.

20 Don't curse the king in your thoughts or demean the rich even in private. If you do, a little bird or other winged creature overhead might overhear and wing your words and report what you said *to those in power*.

Chapter 11

Teacher: *Don't be afraid to* release your bread upon the waters, for in due time you will find it. (Do not be afraid to try your hand at several different disciplines because you never know when one of the skill sets will be useful to you.)

2 Divide your portion—put seven here, maybe eight there—for you can never be sure when or where disaster will strike.

3 When the clouds are *dark and* heavy with rain, showers will fall upon the earth. When a tree falls—whether to the south or the north—it will stay where it lands.

4 Those who watch *and wait* for *favorable* winds never plant, and those who watch *and fret over* every cloud never harvest.

5 You can no more predict the path of the wind than you can explain how *a child's* bones are formed in a mother's womb. Even more, you will never understand the workings of the God who made all things.

6 Get up early to sow your seed, and in the evening find worthwhile things to do, For you never know which will profit you—maybe this, maybe that, maybe both.

--(Side note) Hard work, not idleness, is at the heart of wisdom. (Hard work does not always mean 'working like a dog'. I was taught to work smarter, not harder.) Rewards come when we most need and least expect them. (End note)--

7 Light is sweet; one glimpse of the sun delights the eyes.

8 If a person lives many years, then he should *learn to* enjoy each and every one; but he should not forget the dark days ahead (the dark days is the time that people will not walk this earth), for there will be plenty of them. All that is to come—*whether bright days or dark*—is fleeting. 9 Be happy, *and celebrate all of the goodness of* youth while you are young. Cultivate a cheerful heart every day you have youth. Go where your heart takes you. Take in the sights. *Enjoy,*

but remember that God will hold us accountable for all that we do. 10 *When all is said and done,* clear your mind of *all its* worries. Free your body of *all its* troubles *while you can,* for youth and the prime of life will *soon* vanish.

Chapter 12

1 **Teacher:** *And so we come to the end of this musing over life. My advice to you is to* remember your Creator, *God,* while you are young: before life gets hard *and the injustice of old age comes upon you—* before the years arrive when pleasure feels far out of reach— 2 before the sun and light and the moon and stars fade to darkness and before cloud-covered skies return after the rain. 3 *Remember Him* before the *arms and legs of the* keeper of the house begin to tremble—before the strong *grow uneasy and* bent over *with age*—before toothless gums aren't able to chew food and eyes grow dim. 4 *Remember Him* before the doors are shut in the streets *and hearing fails* and everyday sounds fade away—before the *slightest* sound of a bird's chirp awakens the sleeping but the song itself has fallen silent. 5 People will be afraid of falling from heights and terrifying obstacles in the streets. *Realize that hair turns white* like the blossoms on the almond tree, one becomes slow *and large* like a *gluttonous* grasshopper, and *even caper berries* no longer stimulate desire. In the end, all must go to our eternal home while there are mourners in the streets. 6-7 So before the silver cord is snapped and the golden bowl is shattered: before the *earthen* jar is smashed at the spring and the wheel at the well is broken—before the dust returns to the earth that gave it and the spirit-breath returns to God who breathed it, let us remember our Creator. 8 Life is fleeting; *it just slips through your fingers.* All vanishes like mist.

9 Not only did the teacher attain wisdom by careful observation, study, and setting out many proverbs, but he *was also generous* with

his knowledge and *eagerly* shared it with people. 10 The teacher also searched for just the right words *to bring hope and encouragement,* and he wrote honestly about truth *and the realities of life.*

11 The words of the wise are like goads; the collected sayings of the masters are like the nail-tipped sticks *used to drive the sheep,* given by one Shepherd.

12 So be warned, my child, of anything else that might be said! There is no end to writing books, and excessive study only exhausts the body. 13 And, when all is said and done, here is the last word: **worship in reverence the one True God, and keep His commands, for this is** *what God expects* **of every person**. 14 For God will judge every action—including everything done in secret—whether it be good or evil.

The point is simple, you are getting older. The older that a person gets then the more quickly life seems to pass bye. Before you get caught up in the haste of life take time and consider where we are all headed. Do you really want to spend your life in a manner that will allow you to hold a bag of diamonds at the end. The time that we spend on earth is only a dress rehearsal, just remember that soon it will be opening night!

> *so we come to the end of this musing over life. My advice to you is to remember your Creator, God, while you are young: before life gets hard and the injustice of old age comes upon you—before the years arrive when pleasure feels far out of reach* - Ecclesastes 12:1

Introduction to the Pocket Bible

Every situation is not the same and certain situations might turn out well if they are approached like they are a complex puzzle that needs to be solved in 1,000 moves. But generally speaking I appreciate it when situations can be preformed on a basic level.

That can be a problem when I try to remember how JESUS wants me to behave, but then JESUS taught me about the Pocket Bible. The Pocket Bible allows a person to compress all the pages of the Bible into a file that is much easier to commit to memory! JESUS talked about the Pocket Bible in Matthew 10. I understand that in Mathew 22:34-40 a trap was being set for my KING, but the trap was not even as effective as a strong hand trying to grab a greased pig.

However I was able to understand the question that was asked of JESUS! A Pharisee asked JESUS a question that basicly went like this 'JESUS if you were to take a Bible and put it into a pot of boiling water, and the whole thing was boiled away minis the single most commandment...then what would be left?' (The question was not fair-you-see.) But JESUS answered the question anyway by saying that the greatest commandment was that we should Love the LORD our GOD with all of our heart, soul, and mind and then JESUS told us that #2 was similar to #1. JESUS said the #2 command is that we should Love our neighbor's like we Love ourselves. Then HE said that basicly the entire Bible had been written to explain those two concepts!

Matthew 22:37-40

> *Jesus said to him, " '**You shall love the Lord your God**
> *with all your heart, and with all your soul, and with all*
> *your mind.' This is the first and great commandment. And*
> *the second is like it: '**You shall love your neighbor as***
> *yourself.' On these two commandments hang all the Law*
> *and the Prophets."*

The next time that you see a cross, I want you to note that it is comprised of two beams. The first beam is pointed into the heavens, your first allotment of Love should be sent there! Your second shipment of Love should be sent in the two directions that the horizontal beam points to. And that is the Pocket Bible!

The Church of Jeroboam

Today many churches try to claim some sort of authority by say-ing that they are the 'church of _____'. But most churches are named inappropriately. The sign out front should read 'Welcome to the church of jeroboam.' Of course most people have little to no idea of who jeroboam is mainly because pulpits are filled with hirelings that view preaching as just an occupation and do not know how to instruct there parishioners to study The WORD of GOD because they barely know it themselves. But lets review the convoluted his-tory of the church as told in many churches...actually I do not think that most churches teach any Bible history. Unfortunately, many in the church system are blissfully ignorant, which suits certain pastors well because they could not logical explain why they instruct church members to act a certain way. I guess the modern day history of the church was explained by the song 'tradition' as seen in the movie "Fiddler on the Roof".

But usual the only 'teaching' that the parishioners receive is when the 'pastor' speaks about the children of Israel. Next church members are shown a diagram of the tabernacle/temple. Lastly people are told that GOD no longer desires to dwell in a physical building but GOD chooses to dwell inside the hearts/lives of mankind. But then pastors try to establish a link between the old testament law and the current church system. Well that's the problem, many pastors think that there is a flawless link between the system of worship that was present during the old testament law and how the modern day church operates, but that is not true.

Hebrews 1:1

> *For the law is a shadow of the good things to come, and not the very image of those things....*

Instead of explaining the progression of how GOD has chosen to interact with HIS people, (which the pastor should do) the 'pastor' goes absent without leave and says something like 'a pastor can only do so much'. And its true that a pastor can only do so much, just like good hygiene can only do so much and many other cop outs. It is left up to church goers to correctly piece together the questionable history of the church. It is almost humorous that it is the job of the pastor to help guide church goers, because it is quite evident that some pastors only view the pastorate as a job...and why would a person like that want to strain themselves?. To me a similar comparison would be that we elect government officials so that we do not need to spend every moment reviewing public policy, and then it comes out that the elected officials expect us to continue to send them paychecks even when they are not doing their jobs.

One might think that the lack of leadership that we are experiencing in the church is unprecedented, but let me assure you that the wickedness that is in the church is just a reoccurring theme of church history. To begin this story we will start with the first kings of Israel. First was Saul, next came David, and after him was Solomon. After King Solomon built the first temple and then died, there was a civil war and the nation of Israel split up into two nations. The Northern section of the country appointed there king to be a man named jeroboam, and the southern section of the country had a King named Rehoboam. (Rehoboam was the son of Solomon and was the rightful king over the entire country.) The split was more than an unfortunate occurrence, because the nation was not designed to ruled by the orders of any given man (in a monarchy the king/queen decides what is going to happen). The nation was a Theocracy (that means that GOD was supposed to decide what was going to happen). GOD had already said when, where, and how HE was going to be worshiped and the role of the king was to enforce what GOD said, its sort of like how politicians are not supposed to 'invent' any rules they want instead they should follow the constitution. But after the civil war jeroboam (the northern king) decided that what GOD had said was no longer relevant (that would be like an elected official disregarding the constitution).

1 Kings 12:25-33

> 25 In Israel Jeroboam fortified Shechem in the hilly land of Ephraim. He lived there for a time, then he took on another project and fortified Penuel.

> **Jeroboam said to himself:**

> 26 It is possible that the kingdom might return to the house of David (Rehoboam). 27 If these people make sacrifices in the Eternal's temple in Jerusalem, then their hearts will go back to their lord, even to Rehoboam, Judah's king. <u>They will surely execute me</u> and go back to Rehoboam, Judah's king. 28 The king sought out advice and then cast two calves out of gold.

> **Jeroboam said to Israel:**

> It's too difficult for you to travel all the way to Jerusalem to make your sacrifices. These are your gods, Israel, who

led you out of Egypt. 29 Jeroboam placed one of the golden calves in Bethel and the other in Dan. 30 This was a horribly wicked sin. People even traveled with the golden calf in a religious procession when it was placed in Dan. 31 Jeroboam constructed temples on high places, and he appointed men to be priests who were not descendants of Levi. 32 Jeroboam instituted a festival on the fifteenth day of the eighth month. It was similar to the Feast of Booths that is celebrated in the seventh month in Judah. He then approached the altar in Bethel and offered sacrifices to the golden calves he had crafted. While he was doing this, he instructed the priests of the country's high places to serve in Bethel. 33 Jeroboam then approached the altar in Bethel on the fifteenth day of the eighth month to make sacrifices according to a plan he had devised. There, he instituted this festival for all the Israelites. Then he approached the altar and burned incense.

What happened was that jeroboam realized that if he did not figure out a way to block his followers from worshiping GOD, then the country would once again be united and he would be put to death. To keep his fraud going, jeroboam instituted a three pointed strategy.

1. **Establish a phony heritage**.
2. **Institute an illegitimate priesthood**.
3. **Rearrange the date of observance**.

The **first** thing that jeroboam did was to establish a phony heritage. He did this by secretly moving the capital city. The way the people in ancient Israel thought about things is not the way that we think about things today. For example, by putting a place of worship in a city named 'Bethel' and in 'Dan' (v 29) a false story was being established (Bethel meant house of the LORD and Dan spoke of governmental authority). So in effect jeroboam was deceiving people into thinking that the church that jeroboam had established was endorsed both by GOD and the Government. But in reality the church of jeroboam was a slap in the face of GOD and the entire government was illegitimate.

Today church leaders are still trying to attach a certain names to their clubhouses, but behind all of the smoke its just a company that has a clueless chief executive officer. Funny story, did you know that when JESUS said that HE was going to build HIS church, HE was not even thinking about what we think of as a church. The word that is translated as church was actually -ekklesian-. The word **ekklesia was already hundreds of years old when JESUS used it.** The word was used by the Greek government to described an assembly where citizens would gather and speak about policies. Many, many, many preachers teach that JESUS said that HE was going to establish a building with a pulpit and stain glass windows, but what JESUS actually said was that HE was going to establish HIS system of government! With a belly full of laughter I repeat what Alfred Loisy said:

- JESUS proclaimed the Kingdom of GOD and what came was the church.

(Whaa, Whaa, Whaa)

That would make the church the disappointment of the millennium. Actually the church has been ignoring what JESUS said for over two millennium! It turns out that the only governmental authority that most churches can claim is that the state allows them to count any offerings that they receive as a tax deduction. At best I guess the church could be described as a business, but when the church tries to link up with politics by declaring 501(c)3 status then a new low has been achieved. Many so called pastors are just ceo's, of course some of those ceo's that are standing behind the pulpits are extremely inefficient business men. When the church claims that they are just like every other charity and all of the tithes and offerings should be exempt from taxes, that its a money laundering scheme where the church pimps out the gospel. It would probably be a generous 'church' budget if 10% of the tithes and offerings went to help resolve poverty. The fact that there are many church buildings across this country does not mean the church/clubs have a good business model it just means that some slick tonged charlatan twisted the words of CHRIST! What thoes gospel pimps have done is told people that we need to support the local church/club, but what the club board does not tell people is that the main purpose of the club is to further promote the intrest of the club (and they will put Bibles on the backs of the seats) Its like how the federal reserve is not all that federal, and I think that the only thing that the privately held bank holds in reserve is a printing press. So the name causes people to be misled...I am not so certain that I can say that the federal reserve has nothing to do with the government, but they are about as federal as federal express. The internal parts of the 'church' as well as with the federal reserve, are not the same as what is advertised on the box.

The **second** thing that jeroboam did was he instituted an illegitimate priesthood (v 31). When GOD delivered the children of Israel out of the hand of the Egyptians, the people were divided into tribes. Each of the tries were to preform certain duties, however only the tribe of Levi was to serve as an inter-mediator between GOD and man (it was like that until JESUS said that HE was going to be the only step between GOD and man.) But back to the duties of the Leivites, they were the priestly tribe. GOD gave them no land, they were exempt from military service and they were also excluded from sharing the spoils of war. The lives of the Leivites was to be based around the temple. In fact GOD summed up the lives of the Levites in the book of Numbers.

Numbers 18:21

> *I give to the Levites all the tithes in Israel as their inheritance in return for the work they do while serving at the tent of meeting.* (The tent of meetings was the precursor of the temple)

Today instead of GOD saying who is going to serve HIM, a new system of governance has been elected. Today government officials have appointed certain men and women that claim to be able to dictate the hand of GOD. You might ask how I can claim that the government is responsible for appointing many 'heads' of ministry...well that is what 501(c)3 application is. Most people think that to be in the ministry a person needs to have been hand selected by some sort of ministry board. Receiving credentials from a ministry council or a church board is not how a person is called into the ministry, but the selection process does remind me of some kind of big 'ouija board'. Where else do we see a selection of people huddling together asking an unseen spirit to give an answer? And if a certain minister does not preform according to the satisfaction of the 'church board' then that person is removed from ministry, just like in the mafia.

The **third** thing that jeroboam did was that he rearranged the date of observance.

> *Jeroboam instituted a festival on the fifteenth day of the eighth month. It was similar to the Feast of Booths that is celebrated in the seventh month in Judah.*

It is not hard to see that GOD does not want anyone to think that HE will share HIS spotlight. So by rearranging the date of observance it was kind of like telling GOD 'The appointed time that YOU set to meet with people does not fit into our schedule, so we are going to bump your meeting into a time slot that we find to be more convenient.' In a single sentence 'the church of jeroboam taught people that it was ok to mix Holy things and unholy things together.'

Ezekiel 44:23

> They (the priests) are to teach my people the difference
> between the holy and the common and show them how
> to distinguish between the unclean and the clean.

The sins that Jeroboam had committed was to create a counterfeit religion. Do not think that Jeroboam turned completely away from his heritage, Jeroboam kept a semblance of remaining true to the religious heritage of his people. Verse 28 tells us that he still believed that his people were divinely delivered from slavery in Egypt. Also Amos 8:5 tells us that the church that Jeroboam established in Bethel halfway obeyed god.

Amos 8:5

> Who ask, "When will the new moon festival be done so
> we can sell our grain? And when will the Sabbath end
> so we can sell our wheat? Then we can tamper with our
> scales and make the bushel measure smaller and the
> counterweight heavier to cheat our customers.

Even though the church of jeroboam was a counterfeit church they still acted like they were keeping the commands of god. The church celebrated the new moon festival, and they kept the sabbath.

Christians today are no longer required to live there lives governed by the law of Moses (which was only given to us so that we knew how to reform the part of our character that is easily seen by human eyes). Today Christians are required to live there lives according to the dictates of a much more strenuous law...that is the law of LOVE. (Any knuckle head can sit quietly in church, stand up, clap 3 times, turn around and sit down, but what the KING is looking for is people whose outsides and insides are reformed, and the law of Moses was ineffective at reforming the insides of people.) And the third thing that the church of jeroboam did was, it taught people that people did not need to try to worship GOD like HE said, rather human rules were able to reform the wickedness of the human heart. (The laws of GOD are not just a list of rules that we need to follow, rather they are like a blueprint and if a person does not follow the blueprints exactly like they are laid out then they might as well be working on an entirely diffrent project.)

Romans 8:3

> For what the law could not do, in that it was weak
> through the flesh, God did by sending His own Son in
> the likeness of sinful flesh, and concerning sin, He con-
> demned sin in the flesh

My translation of that verse is: 'The law of Moses set many affairs in order but it was helpless to pin us humans down...do you know why? Its because we are a bunch of rascals. The untamed human heart is so slippery, its like trying to iron a coat hanger! We were hopping around like monkeys, but then GOD sent HIS SON to prove to all of us how to LOVE. I have already explained that many of the so called pastors are shysters that are mainly concerned about the money, but I want to point out that JESUS never did like the religious system. The baboons that stand behind many pulpits try to convince people that JESUS enjoyed pleasant conversations with the religious leaders and that people that had the pleasure of witnessing the display just smiled in amazement.

Luke 2:46-47

> *46 After three days they found him in the temple courts, sitting among the teachers, listening to them and <u>asking them questions</u> (ἐπερωτῶντα). 47 Everyone who heard him was amazed at his understanding and his answers.*

When the WORD says that they were amazed at JESUS understanding, the text should be translated that the people's minds were blown at the level of sophistication and mental complexities of the responses that JESUS gave. The crowds were dumbfounded because this 12 year old boy marched into the temple and when he heard the crap that was being taught then JESUS starts to interrogate the 'preachers' (the phrase 'asking them questions' did not mean that JESUS was seriously wanting advice). The crowd is awestruck by the fact that 'pastor so and so' always gave such put together arguments, but today a young man walked into the temple and started to deconstruct those 'solid' arguments that the temple officials had been feeding folks. People were amazed because the Bible was saying exactly the same thing as what JESUS was saying. Another word to describe what was going on is that people were amazed at the authority that JESUS was operating in! Also do not think that this was an isolated incidence where JESUS just did not get along with the 'church officials'. JESUS and the 'church system' did not get along, in fact it was the church leadership that pushed for JESUS's execution. Right before JESUS voluntarily laid down HIS life, HE was questioned by the 'high priest'. One of the things that I want people to understand is that The WORD of GOD is not just a book that the so called pastor should be preaching. The WORD of GOD is more powerful than a nuclear bomb. The bomb just sits there until it is activated, and that activation comes about when The WORD of GOD is declared. A 12 year old JESUS amazed people because JESUS declared The WORD of GOD and by doing so HE exercised Authority.

(Allow me to digress for a moment.) The true mark of a person of GOD is the Authority, the gauge is not how many times they have read the Bible, or how much Bible trivia that they know. Also I want to briefly mention that JESUS is The WORD of GOD (John 1:14) GOD did not just command us to LOVE, HE knew that we would not understand, so GOD sent JESUS (who is LOVE 1 John 4:7-21) to demonstrate how that we should LOVE...The Muslims say that the Qur'an was sent by Allah via the angel Gabriel. In other words Muslims equate the gift of the Qur'an like Christians celebrate the life of JESUS. I have met some kind Muslims, but I will clearly say that Muslims and Christians do not serve the same God. When the GOD of Abraham, Isaac, and Jacob wanted to teach us how to LOVE then GOD sent HIS SON JESUS...however allah did not even bother to deliver the Qur'an. That is how you feed a diseased dog, I do not even see a small amount of love in allah. I choose to follow the GOD that not only commands me to Love others, but HE also lived a earthly existence that was filled with LOVE! To all of the Muslims I would say that the missing substance in your life is present because allah does not love...in fact allah refers to people as his slaves and not his friends, however JESUS considers HIS followers as friends (John 15:15 *I no longer call you servants, because a **servant does not know his master's business.** Instead, **I have called you friends,** for everything that I learned from my Father I have made known to you.*) Do you realize that I have the privilege of partnering together with the KING! It would be a pleasure to see more people forming such partnerships!

Matthew 8:27

> *The men (disciples) were **amazed** and asked, "**What kind of man is this?** Even the winds and the waves obey him!"*

(JESUS commanded HIS WORDs to come into alignment with the lifestyle that the Bible talks about and the disciples were amazed because they were used to hearing 'pastors' speak one way and live another way. But JESUS was different, suddenly they were seeing the Bible lived **Psalms 95:4-5**).

Matthew 27:54

> Now the centurion, and those who were with him keeping guard over Jesus, when they saw the earthquake and the things that were happening, became very **frightened** (the men were awestruck) and said, **"Truly this was the Son of God!"**

(JESUS had just sacrificed HIS life, and when HE dismissed HIS spirit the earth reacted. A violent earthquake took place and the ground split open. Many people that were followers of LOVE and were already dead and in the grave, some of those people came back to life. At that moment the guards that were present when JESUS died, they heard the earth declare that the KING of everything had just given HIS life **Psalms 24:1**).

Jeremiah 17:9 tells us that the human heart can be very deceptive, and take a look around and you will see that it is true. Human beings are sneaks! Everything appears to be in order on the surface but underneath our skin human hearts are renegades. (People need to stop thinking that the main source of opposition comes from a devil and that the 'church system' is a place where such opposition does not exist. Sometimes I think that some of the strongest opposition that The Kingdom of GOD faces comes from inside of the church.) I recently told a guy that the natural state of mankind is to be selfish, I do not think that he understood what I was saying. Let me make myself clear, many people reject the idea that they need to Love their neighbor...

but some people are so deceitful that they claim to be serving the KING simply because they say that they keep the 'Law of Moses'. Those people try to add offices to the church, create councils, holidays, manners of worship and the like all to hide the fact that they want to love people when they get good and ready. So instead of serving GOD (who is the true King) many people just serve the church. It might sound confusing, but JESUS has already made it easier for us to understand.

Matthew 23:2-4

> 2 *"The scribes and the Pharisees sit in Moses' seat. 3 Therefore, whatever they tell you to observe, that observe and do, but do not do their works. For **they speak, but do nothing**. 4 They fasten heavy loads that are hard to carry and lay them on men's shoulders, but they themselves will not move them with their finger.*

Today we refer to that type of behavior as 'big talk and no action'. JESUS was telling us that within the church system is a group of people that (sort of) tell people how to follow the Bible, we are told that not everything that comes out of the pulpit (Moses' seat) is incorrect but sometimes what is seen in front of the pulpit does not match the actions that go on behind the pulpit.

The sins of Jeroboam was not just an old testament problem. The sins of Jeroboam are still going on today! I am aware that many I am aware that many people think that the Scribes, Pharisees, Sadducees, and Teachers of the Law were bad people, and that misunderstanding probably exists because whoever 'explained' the WORD of GOD to you is an illegitimate hireling that has little business handling the WORD. But the *aforementioned* list of folks would be comparable to preachers, youth pastors, song leaders, and other church leaders. In **Matthew 23:2-4** JESUS explained that the Scribes and Pharisees understood that humans were supposed to look at one another through the eyes of GOD (GOD is LOVE), they just did not want to follow these teachings.

Unfortunately the church leaders of that day became so busy explaining what people were supposed to do, that they forgot to change the way that they were living. The church leaders knew exactly when to stand up, they knew when to clap, those people might have even know when to shout 'Amen', and they wanted other people to preform similar actions. The church of Jeroboam has a case of 'Do as I say, but do not do as I do. Some church goers try to observe religious customs just because they want to belong to the 'church club', we will call those actions 'salvation by proxy'.

The truth is The Kingdom of GOD has a great code of ethics that its members follow, and a person would be crazy if they did not want everyone else to follow the code. The code of ethics is simple to recite and it goes like this "LOVE GOD, and Love mankind". But not many people want to live by that code. I feel that is a decent description of how to travel to The Kingdom of GOD. All humans have received an invitation to be a part of the Kingdom of GOD, but most people stop at the gates of The Kingdom and refuse to pay the admission price to enter. Of course every person has the fare in their pocket, and it does not make good sense to me that more people do not want to pay the price. But I am able to understand why many people think the fare is to pricy...its because the cost of admission is a persons life. Its true that some people are murdered because of there beliefs, but the rest of the citizens of The Kingdom are required to lay down their desires and instead of responding to things the way that I see fit...I am supposed to view life through the eyes of LOVE. Sometimes it almost seems easier to die when we are tasked with viewing the world through the eyes of LOVE. As a citizen of The Kingdom my personal desires should no longer dictate my actions. This concept is demonstrated in a childrens song that I learned when I was younger. The song says 'LOVE is a flag flown high from the castle of my heart'. If you **fly the flag** for your country or a group to which you belong then you represent it or do something to support the cause, but also it means a certain territory is registered to a particular country and sails under its flag. We already know that GOD is LOVE and Kingdom citizens are required to Love **1 John 4:7-8.** So the extremely simple truth is that the castle of my heart (headquarters of my life) no longer flies the flag that says 'Travis!', in other words I have surrendered the territory that I formerly controlled. I am no longer in charge!

Galatians 2:20

> *I have been crucified with Christ; and it is no longer I that live, but Christ liveth in me: and that life which I now live in the flesh I live in faith, the faith which is in the Son of God, who loved me, and gave himself up for me*

I guess some people believe that they have found a 'more worthy' cause to live for. You would think that most people have been able to figure out that the death rate sits at about 100%. A person can get mad but there is no stomping away from GOD.

John 6:66-68

> *66 After this many of his disciples turned back and no longer walked with him. 67 So Jesus said to the twelve, "Do you want to go away as well?" 68 Simon Peter answered him, "Lord, to whom shall we go? You have the words of eternal life*

I have multiple issues with how the church system has twist scripture so it benifiets themselves, but one of the issues is with how the church system deals with finances. Church leaders incorectly teach that 10% of a persons income should be paid to the church. I have already discussed that the the 'church system' has bee turned into a business, and the leadership of many churches function as c.e.o's (chief executive officers) Many of whom I would not trust there financial prowess to preform the most basic of tasks. But I have a larger problem with the teaching that 10% of my income belongs to the LORD. I realize that 100% of my money belongs to the LORD, and GOD wants me to be the executor. How do you think it would reflect on me if I delegated the responsibility that GOD gave to me **Genesis 2:15**, with the knowledge that many, many church officials are financially incompetent. I will not treat GOD like HE is a chump...that's not how you should treat your friends! **John 15:15**

I get the impression that many people assume that anytime that money is mentioned it is a bad thing, but let me assure you that it is the 'love' of money that is the root of all evil. It's like sun exposure. A healthy lifestyle includes moderate sun exposure, but in certain situations sun exposure can be bad. Money is just a tool, it is not good to obsess about money, but its also not entirely healthy to try to live a lifestyle that is completely devoid of anything that money can buy. The ability to manage money will often dictate a persons character.

Matthew 25:14-30

> *Jesus(explained): 14 This is how it will be (an example of how GOD has set up HIS Kingdom). It will be like a landowner who is going on a trip. He instructed his slaves about caring for his property. 15 He gave five talents to one slave, two to the next, and then one talent to the last slave—each according to his ability. Then the*

man left. 16 Promptly the man who had been given five talents went out and bartered and sold and turned his five talents into ten. 17 And the one who had received two talents went to the market and turned his two into four. 18 And the slave who had received just one talent? He dug a hole in the ground and buried his master's money there. 19 Eventually the master came back from his travels, found his slaves, and settled up with them. 20 The slave who had been given five talents came forward and told his master how he'd turned five into ten; then he handed the whole lot over to his master.

Master(said): *21 Excellent. You've proved yourself not only clever but loyal. You've executed a rather small task masterfully, so now I am going to put you in charge of something larger. But before you go back to work, come join my great feast and celebration. 22 Then the slave who had been given two talents came forward and told his master how he'd turned two into four, and he handed all four talents to his master.*

Master(said): *23 Excellent. You've proved yourself not only clever but loyal. You've executed a rather small task masterfully, so now I am going to put you in charge of something larger. But before you go back to work, come join my great feast and celebration.*

24 Finally the man who had been given one talent came forward. **Servant(said):** *Master, I know you are a hard man, difficult in every way. You can make a healthy sum when others would fail. You profit when other people are doing the work. You grow rich on the backs of others.*

25 So I was afraid, dug a hole, and hid the talent in the ground. Here it is. You can have it.

(26 The master was furious.) **Master(said):** *You are a pathetic excuse for a servant! You have disproved my trust in you and squandered my generosity. You know I always make a profit! 27 You could have at least put this talent in the bank; then I could have earned a little interest on it! 28 Take that one talent away, and give it to the servant who doubled my money from five to ten. 29 You see, everything was taken away from the man who had nothing, but the man who had something got even more. 30 And as for the slave who made no profit but buried his talent in the ground? His master ordered his slaves to tie him up and throw him outside into the utter darkness where there is miserable mourning and great fear.*

JESUS tells us that GOD has designed HIS Kingdom to be ran in a certain fashion. To help us understand the rules of the Kingdom JESUS tells us a story. In the story the Master calls three of his servants (understudies) together and explains to them how they are supposed to manage the Masters property. The first two servants preformed well, but the third servant explains that he had reasoned that the best action was to do nothing. The Master became so upset with the insubordination of the servant, that HE had his former servant thrown into hell. (This is when I explain to people that the doctrine that a person can never 'loose their salvation' is a lie! See above scripture and **Romans 11:17-24**) The four main characters in the story was the Master (JESUS), and three servants (Christians). The Master called his servants to himself, and had already determined the ability of each servant (GOD already knows that I am proably never going to preform brain surgery, so GOD is not going to judge me on how good of a surgeon that I am.) The Master delegated a workload to each of his servants. The first servant did not seem to have a difficult time managing what was left in their care...hence the word 'promptly' (v. 16). The second servant sounded like he might have been a little 'slow on the draw', but he got the management job done. I guess the third servant thought that the best way for him to be the manager of his Masters assets was for him to not interfere. (Note: the third servant approached the Gates of The Kingdom but for whatever reason he thought that it would be best if he did not commit to anything).

I do not want people to think that I am advocating the abandonment of all Christian gatherings. I am just trying to point out that a good amount of civic organizations are better suited to act like the church. There are certain pastors that are working hard to teach people to help build the Kingdom of GOD. However, people should probably not be so quick to entrust there tithes and/or offerings to some churches because I feel like some 'pastors' are trying to earn a lifetime achievement award for giving it the 'old college try'.

Isaiah 58:1-7

> ***Eternal One:*** *Tell My people about their wrongdoing; shout with a voice like a trumpet; Hold nothing back: say this people of Jacob's line and heritage have failed to do what is right. 2 And yet they look for Me every day. They pretend to want to learn what I teach, As if they are indeed a nation good and true, as if they hadn't really turned their backs on My directives. They even ask Me, as though they care, about what I want them to be and do, as if they really want Me in their lives.*
>
> *3* ***People:*** *Why didn't You notice <u>how diligently we</u>*

fasted before You? We humbled ourselves with pious practices and You paid no attention.

Eternal One: *I have to tell you, on those (your) fasting days, all you were really seeking was your own pleasure; Besides you were busy defrauding people and abusing your workers. 4 Your kind of fasting is pointless, for it only leads to bitter quarrels, contentious backbiting, and vicious fighting. You are not fasting today because you want Me to hear your voice. 5 What kind of a fast do I choose? Is a true fast simply some religious exercise for making a person feel miserable and woeful* (that sounds like penance)? *Is it about how you bow your head* (like a bent reed), *how you dress* (in sackcloth) (in that culture sackcloth was worn by mourners), *and where you sit* (in a bed of ashes) (sitting in a pile of ashes was the way of showing humility) *Is this what you call a fast, a day the Eternal One finds good and proper? 6 No, what I want in a fast is this: to liberate those tied down and held back by injustice, to lighten the load of those heavily burdened, to free the oppressed and shatter every type of oppression. 7 A fast for Me involves sharing your food with people who have none, giving those who are homeless a space in your home, giving clothes to those who need them, and not neglecting your own family.*

In ancient Israel homelessness was not the same as it is today. Today people might loose their houses because they are on drugs, or they might have committed a crime...there is a number of situations where inviting strangers into your home might be a bad idea. The original hearers of this passage were given a piece of property by

GOD, so if those people ended up homeless then there was a high likelihood that the person was the victim of fraud or deception. Like the fraud and deception of jeroboam which left many Levites without any means to support themselves.

To me, the above passage (*Isaiah 58*) sounds like people were saying to GOD, 'hey GOD we are attending religious services (like fast, and church services) why are YOU not paying attention to what we are doing (by the way GOD LOVES it when people honestly talk to HIM, but your going to get you lunch handed to you when you start thinking that GOD is not doing HIS job). GOD answered them by saying that people thought that they were celebrating GOD, but GOD said that some people are just making noise that they thought sounded nice **1 Corinthians 13:1-8**.

Although mankind is only able to judge the character of a person by trivial matters, GOD judges a person by their true motivations **1 Samuel 16:7**. And the people that are able to impress others, they may or may not be able to impress GOD. In Isaiah 58, GOD looked at how people were trying to impress GOD by preforming a religious ceremony and demanded an explanation. GOD asked if the people thought that HE should be happy with the performance. GOD said that HE is not to impressed that mankind knows how to bow his/her head (like when we pray). GOD is not overly concerned with how a person adorns themselves... even if it is with sackcloth or a three piece suit. Also GOD doe not care where a person sits!

What GOD wants is for us to Love each other! And I will be very clear in saying that Love as it pertains to the Kingdom of GOD is not the same kind of love that the world talks about. Any so called 'church' that has more than two goals or less than two goals...then you should at stop referring to that building as a house of worship. The only two aims that any church should have is to Love GOD and Love mankind. And if any church thinks that it can Love people without some type of action...

those type of people are described in a song by the Supertones 'cut from the branch, fruitless, no good...only one use and that's firewood.'

The Kingdom of GOD is The Kingdom of LOVE!
1 John 4:7-8

The Curse of Jeconiah

It is my belief that most churches do not even preach the entire message of salvation. I did not say that absolutely no one has received salvation. Some people are believers in CHRIST in spite of the antics of 'preachers' (Romans 1:20). The way that things are can be compared to approaching a salad bar, many preachers try to pick and choose what they believe the 'salvation' message should include. At the same time there are a few preachers that try hard to preach the full counsel of GOD.

I want to talk about Jeconiah (there are various ways to spell the name). Many religious institutions fail to teach people that JESUS is the KING. Even though these churches use the word 'King', I do not feel like many people grasp the significance of what they are saying. Allow me to give a truncated history lesson.

GOD objected to the idea that the nation of Israel should have an earthly king (**1 Samuel 8:7**). The reason for this was that GOD was the KING, but GOD finally and gave the people what they wanted and had the prophet appointed a man as king. The man king that was chosen was Saul who was a wicked man, so GOD bailed out the people and appointed David as king. David and GOD got along very well, in fact they got along so well that GOD told David that HE would make sure that the house of David had a forever KING on the throne. After David died one of Davids sons became king (Solomon), and after Solomon died David's grandson Rehaboam became king.

And this went on for about 12 more generations (I expect people to be following along with what I am saying, its in Matthew 1:7-11.) Now the last guy that was listed in Matthew 1:11 was Jeconiah and in keeping with our agreement I am going to talk about him. In the book of Jeremiah chapter 22, GOD records the situation. But the takeaway is that GOD was so disappointed in how Jeconiah was acting as the king that GOD erased the man from history. (Take note that even GOD mocks the idea of 'eternal security' **Jeremiah 22:24** *"As surely as I live," declares the Lord, "even if you, Jehoiachin son of Jehoiakim king of Judah, were a signet ring on my right hand, I would still pull you off.")* Although the story of Jeconiah is interesting, I will move on to the most fascinating part of the story.

Around the time that GOD erased Jeconiah's family from history that was about the same time as GOD allowed another country to invade the land of Judah. **Jeremiah 22:30:**

> *This is what the Lord says:*
> *"Record this man as if childless,*
> *a man who will not prosper in his lifetime,*
> *for none of his offspring will prosper,*
> *none will sit on the throne of David*
> *or rule anymore in Judah."*

In short Judah(Israel) did not have a king for the next 500 years. If you following along, the part of the story that we have just discussed is found in Matthew 1:12-16. History teaches us that the nation of Israel did not flourish without the leadership of a king. (It is interesting to think about how even in modern day times, a human form of government is unable to bring peace to that region. The problem is that a form of government that is totally fair can not exist as long as humans are in control).

Then one day an angel of the LORD visited a man and said that the man was a descendant of king David (more specifically the man was a decedent of Jeconiah) **Matthew 1:20**. If GOD had not wiped out Jeconiah's family line then Joseph would have been king. The way that GOD had designed the story to unfold, the would be 'king' Joseph's great,great...grandfather was king Solomon (this was the branch of the family tree that Israel expected the kings to come from). However GOD had severed the branch of the family tree that contained Solomon (although GOD did allow that branch to be kings... but only for awhile). What GOD had done was that HE rejected the 'kingly line' as it was traced through Solomon and HE installed a new kingly line through Solomon's brother Nathan.

Joseph was betrothed to marry his extremely distant relation. Mary and Joseph were both decedents of king David (But only Joseph was a descendant of Jeconiah). Mary would have been some sort of cousin to Jeconiah (Joseph's family tree is recorded in **Matthew 1:1-16** and the Mary's family tree is recorded in **Luke 3:23-38**). Remember that GOD had told king David that one of his family members was always going to be KING. But GOD also rejected the 'kingly line' and for many years the Jewish people did not understand how GOD was going to keep HIS word. I am pretty confident that you have already figured out how GOD dealt with the 'mystery'! But to recap the events I will say that if JESUS had received any of HIS chromosomes from Joseph then GOD would have violated HIS own decree of wiping the decedents of Jeconiah from the royal family tree. So GOD waited until it looked like it was impossible, and then HE took a dried up stump and made it blossom!

Wow! Lets preach!

Isaiah 11:1-3

1 ***A shoot will come up from the stump of Jesse;*** (Jesse

was the father of king David)

from his roots a Branch will bear fruit.
2 The Spirit of the Lord will rest on him —
the Spirit of wisdom and of understanding,
the Spirit of counsel and of might,
the Spirit of the knowledge and fear of the Lord —
3 and he will delight in the fear of the Lord.

In the above passage GOD is saying that the family tree that king David was apart of, that family tree was going to be cut down and The LORD was going to cause a BRANCH to emerge. Of course that branch was JESUS.

Notice it is within the nature of KING to establish a monarchy and promises the patriarch of that dynasty that his family line will remain in power, then The KING ends the family line and for the next approximately 400 year HE remains silent (a period known as the intertestamental period). GOD did not talk much during the intertestamental period and just when people are thinking that GOD had abandoned Israel suddenly an Angel of the LORD showed up to Joseph and told him that GOD had impregnated his future wife **Matthew 1:20**.

Of course what GOD did was that HE picked Mary to be the birth mother of KING JESUS, but Mary was not just some random girl. Mary's great, great, great, - grandfather was named Nathan (**Luke 3:31**). Nathan was the son of king David, however Nathan was not considered the king instead the king was Nathans brother king Solomon. So the Jewish people thought that the legitimate family tree should follow the decedents of Solomon, but GOD did not like that idea. So GOD established the royal succession through the other brother Nathan. If JESUS was a biological child of Joseph, then GOD would be in violation of HIS own decree that is recorded in **Jeremiah 22:30**.

It just so happens that paganism used to be very popular, so popular that the ancients used to make statues of different pagan gods/goddesses. Which helped out the early institutionalized 'church' because the early 'church' representatives capitalized on the pagan statues. The early 'church' representatives piggybacked on stories that already existed within the culture so statues of the pagan goddess Isis and her son were renamed to be 'The virgin Mary and the Son of God'.

In an ironic turn of events, pagan religions almost got back at some of the church 1000 years later when Santeria was tied to 'Christianity'. For the people that are unfamiliar with Santeria, I will explain. Back in the 16th century, slaves were transported from Western Africa into the Caribbean area. Of course the slaves used to have a different life along with different religious practices. Suddenly they were told that they were no longer able to practice religion like they had been accustomed to, so rather than abandon they religions that they had practiced in Africa...a blending occurred. I know of a guy that used to be involved in Santeria, and I watched a video where the guy went into a shop that had statues of religious significance and it was explained that people purchase the religious trinkets but an evil spirit has been assigned to the object.

Since Santeria is less organized and does not have any 'official religious text' it can be tricky to follow what has been done, but below are two examples of what has been done:

- Followers of The Catholic teachings understand who Saint Christopher was. He supposedly helped a small child by carrying them across a river, so within the Catholic mindset St. Christopher is the patron saint that oversees not only boatmen but also all travelers. However, the organizers of the Santeria religion took the 'spirits' that they were used to worshiping (because they were followers of the Yoruba religion) and hid them behind images of St. Christopher. In the Yoruba tradition there is a spirit known as 'aganyu', its true that spirit is the territorial demon that is in control of volcanoes and earthquakes but the spirit is said to have once worked on a ferry. And since the founders of Santeria were 'forced' to not worship that territorial demon, the switch was made and they started referring to 'aganyu' as St. Christopher.

Many 'preachers' and 'church leaders' have completely dropped the ball and do not teach what the Bible says. I realize that many people are lured towards the New Age teachings of meditation and yoga (which are designed to attract to you a 'spirit guide' but what is going on is that people are inviting territorial spirits into there lives). The ironic part is that if 'churches' would start to preach the WORD of GOD then I believe the New Age teachings would be more vacant. To quote a former priest in the church of satan 'I stopped preforming which craft when I found out that he (the mans 'spirit guide') was on the loosing team'. Please read **Daniel 10**. The Bible explains to us that when a person prays then GOD might hear us, but the answer to our prayer request might be captured by enemy forces. In the story that we are discussing Daniel (the same guy that was formerly in the lions den) prayed to GOD and GOD sent the answer to be delivered by an angel. While the angel was on his/her delivery route, the angel was hijacked by a territorial demon that is called 'the prince of Persia'. **Daniel 10:13** says that 'the prince of Persia' would not let that (good guy) angel pass, and the standoff lasted for 21 days. At last, the angel Michael joins the conflict and the messenger is allowed passage to deliver the message. But that was not the end of if. After the message is delivered, the angel announces that he has to go back the way that he came. And when the angel rejoins the conflict then the 'demon prince of Persia' was going to call for back up **Daniel 10:20**. At that point this angel and Michael would be battling two territorial spirits

(#1 the prince of Persia, #2 the prince of Greece) **Daniel 10:21.** But the part that I think that many people will find interesting are the words spoken in the next verse. **Daniel 11:1** explains to us what a human being can do to take part in the unseen spirit world (remember I told you that GOD has made it possible for each of us to take join HIM when we live like HE directs us).

- The second example that I want to use to explain of how Santeria has intermingled with parts of Catholicism is St. Lazarus or Lazarus of Bethany. Lazarus was a guy that was dead, but then JESUS made him undead. I do not know why but some people teach that if a person is sick and is in need of restoration or is stuck by poverty and is in need of a helping hand then those people should ask for the mercy of a guy that died. But that is what some people believe, and around the 16th century this belief was forced onto followers of the Yoruba religion. So what was done was that the slaves started to see how Lazarus was like a demonic spirit that they called 'babalu aye'.

The majority of church goers might think that I am only discussing information that is relevant in fairy tales. But I am going to declare that once again a foul spirit has been permitted to enter into the camp. The vileness has gone largely unopposed because the 'preachers' have fallen asleep while on guard duty! Do not think that I am saying that a vile spirit has slipped in trough a crack in the wall, this spirit has paraded through the main gate. Perhaps you have heard of a show that was called 'I love Lucy'. There was an actor that played on that show, his name was Desi Arnaz (Ricky). Are you aware that that actor preformed a song for the demonic spirit 'babalu aye'. The show has been archived and a person is able to watch the clip from the shows Ricky preforming the ballad. The title the show clip has been filed under is 'badass babalu'. One of the things that is disturbing about the clip is that as Ricky beats the drum (look up drumming circles and whichcraft). While Ricky sings and dances in commemoration of that foul spirit, he seems to transforms into what I would say is 'not himself'. Let me assure the reader that the spirit world is very active today and you do not have the choice to just sit on the side lines. If you do not stand on the side with GOD (and vote for GOD with your actions), then by default you will cast your vote for mammon

The Challenge of Lordship

The church has this weird God complex, and they seem to have difficulties understanding that they are not GOD. If a person took time to discover what the Bible actually said then the organized church system would realize that the only devil that people need to deal with can be found in a mirror. Here is a news flash for many in the church system...GOD LOVES people, and when the devil starts bad mouthing people that makes GOD mad. I do not know what kind of stunt that the church system is trying to pull, but GOD LOVES us more than a grizzly bear love her cubs and GOD will not tolerate some foul mouthed devil talking trash about HIS kids. But I guess that they have never read **Revelation 12:10**.

I am uncertain why the church teaches people that somehow we need to overcome satan, but let me settle the identity crisis that the church system is involved in. The enemy of JESUS is satan (but the victory of that battle has already been recorded in **Revelation 12:11**). The enemy of people is the temptation of 'falling in love with the pleasures that this world has to offer' and **James 1:14** says that the source of our grief is already between our ears. So the fact that the 'church' is busy 'stomping the devil out' reminds me of the foo fighters of WWII.

The church does not seem to understand that the only part of the devil that is able to function is the mouth. The devil is the accuser of the brethren. The devil is the enemy of CHRIST, the enemy of human beings is our fleshly desires. That means that the devil keeps trying to disfigure the work of CHRIST by talking trash. The devil is working to destroy the work of GOD and it is frustrating that the church thinks it is there job to mount a counter attack? **Colossians 2:14-15** explains that JESUS already bundled all of the accusations that the devil could throw at us and nailed them to the Cross. JESUS already knocked out the teeth of every devil and then HE challenged them all to a steak eating contest! Even though what JESUS did is humorous and make me very proud, the feelings are quickly snuffed out when I am reminded of the pathetic message that most of the church preachers teach. They act like it is their spiritual obligation to get into a fist fight with the devil. The only power that satan has is the power that has been temporarily gifted to him by GOD (The KING).

Most of the people that go to church are taught that the church and satan are somehow locked in a battle. The Bible tells us that not only did JESUS incapacitate all of hell, but then HE made a spectacle out of every devil. Then the church has the nerve to teach that 'we need to watch out for those hellish lions'. I am tired of seeing the Bible butchered by people that claim to be teachers of Gods Word. Many churches like to point to **1 Peter 5:8** and teach people that 'the devil is our adversary and he is waiting to gobble us up'. I am uncertain as to what part of not having teeth is so hard to understand, I sometimes get the feeling that some preachers do not even try to understand what the KING has said. Don't they realize that satan is already a defeated adversary, to ensure the defeat of the devil in our lives all we need to do is submit to GOD. Let me make it simple, "whenever satan comes and suggests that you follow your own desires, then all that you need to do is what the Bible says!". The enemy roars because that's about all he can do. What needs to be understood is that the word 'adversary' is talking about a political rival.

The position that many churches have taken can be described

by an online game that I played. The point of the game was to fire weapons at the other players. In one of the battles that I was playing someone fired a sticky bomb that hit another player. Immediately the player tried to run away from the sticky bomb, but the bomb was already stuck to him. The player was unable to outrun the bomb that had been thrown at him because the bomb had already became a part of him. In a similar manner it is both pathetic and humorous when the church teaches that they need to stomp the devil. Its pathetic because JESUS already told us that HE has already secured victory over the hordes of hell, but at the same time its funny because who would want to be on a team that wants to stomp on each other! If you want to get a good look at a devil, then you should look in the mirror. As we are told in the book of **James 1:14 "each person is tempted when they are dragged away by their own evil desire and enticed."** The devil might have suggested the act but you were a willing participant.

In any conflict it is imperative to identify the enemy, and JESUS made it clear in **Matthew 6:24** that *'it is not possible for anyone to be in the service of two masters'* and then JESUS names the two choices that people have, and guess who JESUS did not mention...thats right it was wimpy the lion! The credible threat that believers face is the temptation to fall in love with this world (wealth).

Mathew 6:24

> *No one can serve two masters; for either he will hate the one and love the other, or he will be devoted to one and despise the other. You cannot serve God and wealth.*

Many people are living a hellish lifestyle, but a person should exercise caution when saying 'so and so follows satan' because 'so and so might just be following their own comfort' (looking out for #1 is serving wealth). Many 'church' leaders have fabricated a story where they teach individuals that 'we need to do battle with the devil'. What should be taught is that many people need to learn 'self restraint'. My assumption is that many people will lose some weight and other problems will vanquish if more people learned that the enemy had already planted thoughts in there heads.

The Bible tells that the first thing that we are doing wrong is that we are trying to manage our stress and anxiety by ourselves. Hearing the roar of a lion will cause anxiety (**1 Peter 5:8**), therefore we are to just surrender our anxiety to GOD. The second problem with what the church teaches is that it fails to mention to 'the parishioners' that they can not effectively battle satan because there is to much fraternizing with the enemy. **John 3:30** says *"HE (GOD) must increase, but I must decrease"*, people need to realize that human nature is at war with GOD.

1 Peter 5:7-8

> 7 <u>casting all your care upon Him</u> *(The KING), for He cares for you.*

> *8 Be sober, be vigilant; because your adversary the devil walks about **like a roaring lion, seeking whom he may devour.***

It is bad that the church has instructed people to fight there own reflections, and it is a very sad position. The sad reality of not properly identifying the enemy is two fold. The first issue is that many people that claim to be a part of the Body of CHRIST are helplessly thinking that they need to defeat there own shadows, meanwhile the real enemy is not being talked about (and the real enemy is preferring the things of this world more than living for GOD. This is what we should be fighting to keep away from). The second issue is that while the church is busy pointing out how a person can 'improve themselves', the important message that satan wants to overthrow GOD is not being preached. So the 'church' has earned a double failing grade. I think that a tv show was made that talked about how the church is preaching The Gospel of The Kingdom...wait, no I was thinking about the show 'The Biggest Looser'.

(Please allow me to teach some history that is laid out in the Bible)

Lets just go ahead and start at the beginning of mankind. Most of us know the story of how Adam and Eve were deceived into not following the instructions that GOD gave them. Mankind choose to not follow the instructions, and GOD let mankind do what we wanted to do (that is what free will is). As a result of mankind's decision pain and suffering entered into the world. GOD gave the first prophetic WORDs in the Bible when HE looked at the devil and said that satan (the serpent) was going to strike at the heel of the woman, but the woman's seed is going to crush the head of the serpent. (Please compare **Genesis 3:15** with **Revelation 12:1-6**)

I was going to say that most church systems actually do a good job teaching the WORD of GOD (As long as the sermons stay within the first three chapters of the Bible.) But I am not going to stretch the truth. What I feel fairly confident in saying is that the church system does a pretty good job when it comes to teaching the first verse of the Bible. Many church leaders are so clueless that they are not even able to see the 'Trinity' in verses 2-3, but let me explain.

Genesis 1:2-3

> *2 The earth was without form, and void; and darkness was on the face of the deep. And the Spirit of God was hovering over the face of the waters. 3 Then God said, "Let there be light"; and there was light.*

In the beginning, GOD The FATHER, GOD The SON, and GOD The HOLY SPIRIT were presiding over all the molecules **(v. 2)**, but nothing happened until GOD The SON spoke up **(v. 3)**. The next event that happened was what I call the 'big bang theory' of creation...GOD has always been present and when The WORD (JESUS CHRIST is the SON of GOD and HE is also the WORD **John 1:1-5**) spoke up then came the -B.A.N.G- and all this stuff was produced. I feel as if this entire book that I have written can be summed up with the correct interpretation of **John 1:5**.

John 1:5

> *The light* (JESUS CHRIST is the LIGHT) *shines in the darkness* (before GOD the SON spoke the world was dark and chaotic and the darkness and chaos was resisting Order from happening), *and* **the darkness can never extinguish it.**

John 1:5 explains the situation well. If you want to understand why the KING came to earth, John 1:5 says that the darkness was trying to suppress the work that the KING wanted to accomplish, and so The KING came to earth to straighten out all the confusion. People were confused because they though that they had to serve 'the unforgiving god' (mammon). The first thing that JESUS did when HE started HIS earthly ministry **Matthew 4:12-14** was to move to a small fishing village in the Northern section of Israel. I want to point out why JESUS did this when HE heard that John the Baptist had been placed into prison. We are told why JESUS acted the way HE did and **Isaiah 9:1-2** is referenced. In the Isaiah passage we find out that The KING made it HIS first priority to go deliver a message of hope to people that were living in 'gloomy darkness' (which was a situation that appeared to be hopeless). Finaly a few months later The KING gets around to addressing John the Baptist **Matthew 11:5** and the question that John wants to ask JESUS is found in Matthew 11:3.

Matthew 11:3

> ...*Are you the one who is to come* (Are you the the MESSIAH that is going to rescue Israel), *or shall we look for another?*

JESUS did not say anything about HIS death, burial, or resurrection, also the concept of salvation was not addressed. Instead JESUS did not address the side issues, what the KING did was said how HE was making a mockery out of hopeless situations (**v. 5**...people that are blind, lame, have leprosy, the deaf, and the dead people – all of thoes people have been caught up in a situation that has been dubbed 'a hopeless situation' and in each of thoes situations The KING has over ruled. Now every situation that 'the powers of this world' thought that they were in control of has been voided out.) Then in verse 6 JESUS states that it is possible to get so focused on all the things that 'Salvation' means, that a person might actually stumble over the ONE who gives Salvation.

Matthew 11:4-6

> *4 Jesus replied, "Go back and report to John what you hear and see: 5 The blind receive sight, the lame walk, those who have leprosy are cleansed, the deaf hear, the dead are raised, and the good news is proclaimed to the poor. 6 Blessed is anyone who does not stumble on account of me."*

Why would someone become offended/stumble on account of CHRIST? To be clear the word that was used was σκανδαλισθῇ, and the word means 'to entice to sin' or 'entice to sin to the point of apostasy'. So JESUS was saying to John 'bonus points shall be given to the people that accept the salvation message and then do not loose there salvation because The KING is not about what they think.' I have already explained that many first century individuals who were waiting for The KING to arrive, were offended once they found out that The KING was not who they expected The KING to be.

(Perhaps some people are in disbelief that a believer can forfeit there salvation. Let me clearly say that many people have been lied to because the Bible teaches that someone can accept salvation and then go astray...**Matthew 25:30, Luke 8:13-14**.)

Now, lets look at flaws in what the church system teaches on day two of creation.

The Bible teaches us that we exist inside a pocket of air. **Genesis 1:6** records that GOD placed the air bubble between the waters. In my experience the majority of 'church leadership' does not have a proper understanding of the earth that GOD has created. GOD has placed over our heads the 'floodgates of heaven' (**Genesis 8:2**). Next time some slick eared preacher tries to explain to you that the only thing that is above a persons head is air, that preacher needs to learn that we live inside of a terrarium, **Genesis 1:6** calls the air pocket that we live in a vault (New International Version).

Another mishandling of scripture that the church system teaches can be read about in **Genesis 1:16-17**. By the time that we are done reading what the Bible actually says, what the institutionalized church teaches will be exposed for the pathetic joke that it is. The Bible explains that GOD created <u>two</u> lights and placed them <u>inside the vault</u>, the fact that the preachers have jumped into bed with people that teach evolution really bothers me! (The theory of evolution is just the second half of the lie that tries to explain a 'Creatorless creation'. The first part of the theory is called 'the big bang'...and I already explained how that the 'big bang' was 'voice activated'.) Allow me to repeat what the Bible says, 'GOD created two lights. What the Bible does not teach us is that GOD made 1 light (the sun) and 1 reflector (the moon). I do not know how preachers think that the moon has a dark side (maby they think that the moon is like a one sided light bulb).

Another important nugget of truth that the preachers fail to mention is that the creation that is taught by main-stream science and the creation that GOD made are two extremely different models. For reasons that are not being discussed at this time, almost 99% of the preachers that I know of teach the model that GOD is not responsible for. The preachers 'explain' that the sun is far away from the earth, and that the moon rotates around the earth. However the Bible explains that GOD placed both of the _lights_ inside the vault **v. 17**, GOD also placed the stars inside the 'air' vault.

Science says that the stars are distant mini suns. It makes me wonder why people do not wear sun glasses at night? If you have ever viewed a star through a telescope you will quickly see that stars are in no way distant suns. (Also if you check the temperature of the moon light, you will find that the light is cold. However if you measure the temperature of the light that the sun gives, you will find that the light is hot. Logic dictates that night and day have two different light sources.)

You gotta hand it to GOD because HE wrote a book that destroys the scientific model of the universe. **Genesis 1:20** records GOD as placing living birds that could fly across the vault of the sky. So I am not sure where 'the moon landing' took place, but supposedly they landed on a structure that was only able to reflect the sun and living things could not survive (without a special suit). I think that it would be neat to watch a man step foot on the moon with a parrot on his shoulder.

Of course the convoluted tale grows deeper when people find out that the 'nasa' space program was organized by a group of former natzi's. I think the question is 'where did nasa land'. I do not suppose that there is a real short way for me to say what I need to say, but I will try! The natzi party was heavily involved in the occult. Many preachers do not explain the Bible, because they do not even understand the Bible. In **Revelation 2:13** GOD was referring to an actual city that was home to a pagan temple to 'zeus'. GOD referred to the temple as *"the seat of satan"*. The natzi party had the temple taken apart and re-assembled at their head quarters in Berlin. I believe that a case could be made that says that 'the space race' was an attempt to reach a dimension that has access to the dimension where GOD's thrown exists **Daniel 11:38-39**. That would mean that the current church leaders that are supporting the unholy claims about celestial bodies not being where GOD said they were, it almost appears like we have a modern day tower of babel.

Like I said most churches understand that GOD created everything that we see, unfortunately most do not realize that GOD is actively involved with the management of life on earth and that we are currently witnessing an attempted coup that is taking place in the spiritual realm. Although what the church system is doing is working to discredit GOD (and it appears that the church system is acting like a cheer leader for the malevolent forces), we are going to step past those misdeeds and explore the Biblical story that many, many churches fail to mention. (Although do no be misled into thinking that GOD is going to wink at being discredited!)

Most churches teach that **Genesis 6** is just the beginning part of the story about Noah and the ark, but that is an understatement. **Genesis 6:4** explains that human beings were not the only creatures that humanoid creatures that called earth home. A humanoid that is known as the Nephilim were trying to crowd out the creation that

GOD had placed on the earth. GOD said that HE was going to clear the board and repopulate the earth through Noah. So the flood story can also be thought of as the flush story!

Genesis 6:1

> When human beings (#1) began to increase in number on the earth and daughters were born to them, 2 the sons of God (#2) saw that the daughters of humans were beautiful, and they (#2) married any of them (#1) they chose. 3 Then the Lord said, "My Spirit will not contend with humans (The original Hebrew does not say humans, but should proably be translated as GOD saying "MY SPIRIT will not contend with 'fleshly bodies') forever, for they are mortal; their days will be a hundred and twenty years." 4 The Nephilim were on the earth in those days—and also afterward—when the sons of God went to the daughters of humans and had children by them. They were the heroes of old, men (Champions) of renown (like Hercules). 5 The Lord saw how great the wickedness of the human race had become on the earth (#1 had been corrupted by #2), and that every inclination of the thoughts of the human heart was only evil all the time. 6 The Lord regretted (was grieved in HIS heart) that he had made human beings on the earth (#1), and his heart was deeply troubled. 7 So the Lord said, "I will wipe from the face of the earth the human race I have created—and with them the animals, the birds and the creatures that move along the ground—for I regret that I have made them." 8 But Noah found favor in the eyes of the Lord. 9 These are the records of the generations of Noah. Noah was a righteous (Noah was 100% human) man, blameless

in his time (The genealogy of Noah said that he was a pure blooded human); *Noah walked with God.*

At this point it is painfully obvious that 99.995% of preachers do not even attempt to interpret the Bible correctly. Instead they just regurgitate a similar sounding message as the next charlatan. They invite people to attend their church services, and they say that there is a Biblical precedent. The question that I will ask is 'Why do them snakes expect people to listen to them talk about scripture when it is obvious that they do not even understand what they are trying to peddle?'

Like GOD said, the great flush just wiped the Nephilim from the earth (at that time) but it did not get rid of the humanoids. You might be asking, 'If everything that was not in the ark died does that mean that the Nephilim somehow survived'? No they died, but its like the chorus of the song 'the cat came back'. People need to understand who the Nephilim were. **Genesis 6:2** tells us that the Nephilim were produced when the sons of GOD (also see Job 6:1) took part of stuff from mortal man (like when GOD took Adams rib and made Eve). GOD took part of Adam and that was the foundation for Eve to be made with. The Bible indicates that 'the sons of GOD' almost abducted women and intermingled with them. Basicly the Nephilim were part human and part supernatural being (Like Hercules. His mother was a human being, but his dad was zeus) It is interesting to study how the Nephilim desperately want a carbon based life form to inhabit **Matthew 8:28-31**.

Its pretty evident that those fallen angles took human D.N.A. and tried to intermingle it with there own 'D.N.A'. To be clear what they did was that they took the spirit (the brain and emotions) of a fallen angel *"The sons of GOD"*, and they mixed it with a human bod, as a result a humanoid was created. The body of the humanoid was difficult to kill but the internal mechanism could not be destroyed. The creatures that the fallen angles meshed together were called the Nephilium. The fallen angels thought that they were smart enough to make 'Humanity 2.0', but JESUS explained that it is a terrible experience to not be in possession of a biological earth suit **Matthew 12:43**.

Genesis 6 is the beginning part of the drama that is told throughout the Bible. And it so happens that a large percentage of the church system, does not have a baseline knowledge of what the Bible teaches. The basic story goes like this satan is constantly trying to prove that he is 'better than GOD'. The satan is not able to create anything (other than lies) but the devil wants to prove that he has a plan that is better than GOD's plan. That little pervert does not want to become like GOD, that twisted critter thinks that he has a shot at putting GOD to shame **Isaiah 14:14**

It is patheticly humerus to listen to people whine saying 'GOD must not be fair because HE ordered the excision of entire clans of people' **Deuteronomy 20:17**. First of all they were not even human (Yep the promised land was Nephilim headquarters). **Numbers 13:23-29** is proof of the fact that the promised land was not a human civilization. And secondly when GOD says something, then don't question the validity of the statement.

It is my belief that after the flood/flush, those illicit humanoids were invited back to earth through 'witchcraft' (or the occult) **Genesis 10:8-10**. **1 Chronicals 1:10** says that Nimrod (who was the great grand son of Noah) started to become 'a mighty man' sort of like what we read about in **Genesis 6:4**. It sort of does not matter 'how' the Nephilim came back, because GOD tells us that the Nephilim were on the earth after the flood.

I would like to share some information that a number of preachers have probably not spoken. In **Genesis 11:1-9**, the fact that the original language that was used in that instance was _Akkadian_ is not discussed. A large section of the Old Testament was written in Hebrew. The Bible named the tower that Nimrod was constructing 'The tower of babel'. The tower was named babel because of how GOD ended the project. But in the minds of the people of that day, the 'the tower of babel' was not being built (that is what it is called in the Hebrew language). In Akkadian the were building what was called the 'the gate of the gods' (We would call it a star gate). On side 'A' was the earth but when you stepped through the portal you was in a different dimension. Perhaps 'the space race' is actually 'the inter dimensional race'. I feel that way because whatever they 'former nazi's' landed on was not the moon. This information is abit unnerving because **Daniel 11:39** explains to us that without the 'interdimensional portal' the antichrist would not be able to attack the STRONGEST FORTRES.

I thought that I already pointed out the fact that the church system might be mentioned in the Bible. In the Greek mindset when you see someone depicted as having horns you probably should not think 'wa-ha that guy is wearing devil horns'. In Greek architecture 'horns' generally represented power/authority. So when we read in **Revelation 13:11** that a man comes fourth from the earth and the man is described as having "two horns like a lamb and he spoke like a dragon". The way that I interpret what is going on is that a man that looks like a lamb (speaking of the LAMB OF GOD) but having the voice of a dragon (In **Revelation 12:9** that dragon is identified as satan, or the first person in the un-holy trinity of the anti-christ system). Couple that with the fact that it sort of appears like there are other motivating factors behind 'the space race'. Ironically (which has nothing to do with 'Iron' or "Rocks") I think **Daniel 11:36-39** is talking about the un-holy trinity. I think the question needs to be asked 'Is the church system helping to clear the way so that the un-holy trinity can arrive'?

Maby I have not done the best job at driving the point home, but satan is a copy cat. That evil creature is behind many counterfeits. And people need to be taught about that, but the church system is in my opinion receiving a failing grade. GOD makes humans then the copy-cat fuses together the Nephilim. In **Revelation 19:11** CHRIST rides in on a white horse, well guess what color horse satan wants **Revelation 6:2**. I have already explained about how the punk formed the unholy trinity. I think that just like GOD created Wisdom before HE did anything else, satan's hype 'woman' is woman folly.

The 'tower' in the tower of babel was not the main attraction, the main attraction was what was placed on top of the 'tower'. A religious shrine, or 'the gate of the gods' was to be placed at the top of the tower. Its interesting to learn about what the Myan religion says about 'quetzalcoatl'. But if you want to get an idea of what the tower of babel might have looked like, all that you need to do is look at 'el castillo' in Chichen Itza, Mexico.

An extremely pivotal chapter in the story of kingdoms of earth is **Daniel 11**. In that chapter we are told about the personalities of four different 'kings'. The four 'kings' are spread through time, but they are all from the same gene pool. The four 'kings' are related through a 'spiritual bond'. I am aware that many people probably attend some kind of 'church' that has taught 'little to nothing' about the antichrist, but the Bible does not leave us in the dark. In **Daniel 11** we are told that over the course of the entire human existence that there was going to be four 'antichrist models'. The way that GOD designed things the fourth one was going to be really ugly and have all the bad habits of the first three.

I want to mention that in my mind three of the anti-christ models have already come and gone, and of course the fourth one is the one that many people know as the anti-christ. Perhaps you picked up on the words that I used, *the fourth one was going to be really ugly and have all the bad habits of the first three*...that is important. The question becomes 'what negative trait did the first three have'? I should mention that I think the first three were: #1 Nimrood, #2 Antiochus Epiphanes, and #3 Adolph Hitler. What is the greatest objectionable characteristic that all three have in common, well they all tried to fashion some sort of pathway so that they could enter GOD Almighty throne room and challenge HIM. (Nimrood worked at the tower of babel, Antiochus Epiphanes tried to work at the Tempel before it was destroyed, and Adolph Hitler was was working on 'Die Glocke' and moving the seat of satan to Berlin Germany.)

So in a way I feel that nasa was not going into 'outer space' rather they were trying to tunnel through 'inter-dimensional space' (Kind of like what c.e.r.n. is doing.). I tend to think that in **Revelation 13:1** we will see part of the anti-christ system appearing out of the sky sea. Remember in **Genesis 1:6-7** we learned about the body of water that is above the sky. I know that many 'preachers' have not taught people that the 'sea' is above the sky, but maby the sky sea is the location of the entrance of the anti-christ system? If the anti-christ system does come out of the sky sea it would probably look like an alien invasion! So perhaps nasa is 'working' to establish a path that goes between the human realm and the spiritual realm. The rabbit hole gets a little deeper when you figure out that in 'Egyptology' the moon is said to represent the missing left 'eye of horus'. So on numerous fronts I think that the preachers should stop celebrating the fact that 'we landed on the moon'.

I guess some Bible teachers just hurry past the parts of the Bible where GOD orders the Jewish people to wipe a certain culture out, but the truth is that the promised land was not even occupied by humans. GOD lead the children of Israel out of slavery in Egypt into the promised land, but it was only sort of an invading army...mainly the

Israelite's acted like exterminators.

Deuteronomy 7:1-3

> As the Eternal, your True God, is bringing you into the land
> where you're going to live when you cross the Jordan,
> He'll drive out many nations ahead of you—Hittites,
> Girgashites, Amorites, Canaanites, Perizzites, Hivites, and
> Jebusites—seven nations that are bigger and stronger than
> you are. 2 The Eternal your God will put them in your
> power. You must crush them; destroy them completely!
> Don't make any treaties with them, and don't show them
> any mercy. 3 Above all, don't intermarry with them! Don't
> marry your daughters to any of their sons, and don't marry
> your sons to any of their daughters.

I think that it is interesting that native Americans tell stories of giant 'people' that had 6 fingers on each hand. King David had a group of mighty men that killed 'giant' men that had 6 fingers on each hand an (**2 Samuel 21:16, and 1 Chronicles 20:6-8**) that's a new way to think of the Indian greeting.

I am skipping over some very interesting and important history so that the part that are most interesting can be highlighted. People need to know that many 'church services' are led by individuals that barely know what is going on, its like the blind leading the blind! Many churches teach the story that's easiest for them to tell, just do not expect to understand many events if the only people that you listen to have the prefix 'rev.' in front of there name. I believe that people need to have at least a basic understanding of Biblical history, and then once that foundation is laid the end times events will become more clear.

As has been shown, in Biblical terms 'snakes' represent the bad guys and there is going to be a really big and really ugly snake. And the snake is going to be involved in a battle where he will seek to destroy the descendant of the human, but the one who became flesh and blood will utterly destroy the serpent, just like **Genesis 3:15** says. Like I tried to explain before, GOD gave the biggest 'spoiler alert' when HE said that. GOD foretold the 'main conflict' in an ongoing battle. Pretty much from that point onward 'snakes/serpents' normally had something to do with evil or the devil. Anyway **Genesis 3:15** talked about many Biblical events, but the event that I want to land on is found in **Revelation 12**. Also I want to point out that according to the Myan religion 'quetzalcoatl' is the deity that was known as the Plumed Serpent, also the deity was known as 'kukulkán'.

Revelation 12:14

> *The woman was given the two wings of a great eagle,*
> *so that she might fly to the place prepared for her in the*
> *wilderness, where she would be taken care of for **a time,***
> ***times and half a time** (thats 3 1/2 years, just like the 3*
> *1/2 years that the pre-trib rapture theory says that people*
> *will miss), out of the <u>serpent</u>'s reach.*

It seems to me that **Revelation 13** talks about a 'new' infestation of planet earth. (In a later section, I describe how I think that in Revelation 13:1 describes a potential 'alien' invasion. The nephilim do not die like human beings do. **Genesis 6** did not say there was giants and then the flood wiped everything out except the giants. The nephilium are like a bad weed that you stomp on and grind under foot yet they come back. The nephilium 'spirits' just hang around waiting for a body to possess. Rather than thinking that the nephilium die like humans do, for them 'death' is more like them being evicted from the human suit that they are occupying. Now them spirits hate to be hung out to dry (so they want to possess a person) And if they are unable to possess a person, the next best thing for them is an animal host (**Mark 5:1-11**)

Matthew 8:28-32

> *28 When He came to the other side into the country of the Gergesenes, there met Him two men possessed with demons, coming out of the tombs, extremely fierce, so that no one might pass by that way. 29 Suddenly they cried out, saying, "What have we to do with You, Jesus, Son of God? Have You come here to torment us before the time?" 30 Now a good way off from them was a herd of many swine feeding. 31 So the demons begged Him, saying, "If You cast us out, permit us to go away into the herd of swine." 32 He said to them, "Go!" And when they came out, they went into the herd of swine. And suddenly the whole herd of swine ran violently down a steep place into the sea, and perished in the waters.*

In the passage discussed above, JESUS is walking along and HE came across a 'man' that had an unclean spirit (Strongs Concordance says that the man had a spirit that was mixed). The man that JESUS met had a mixed spirit. To give people an idea of how a mixed spirit operates, a mixture is a combination of at least two things. So the man that had a mixed spirit was not totally human. The Bible tells us that several attempts were made to try to subdue this thing and even iron chains could not hold back the things strength. (I want to point out that **1 Corinthians 11:10** speaks of women covering there heads due to the *angels* (Or supernatural beings; was there a debate that questioned if a woman could remain uncovered without attracting 'the sons of GOD?). I know I am in the middle of a conversation that is talking about an encounter that JESUS had in the book of

Matthew, but people need to hear the WORD of the LORD. A large number of preachers/pastors are illegitimate and do not attempt to teach people the entire counsel of GOD's WORD. When I mention some scriptures it might sounds like I am fabricating scriptures, but I do not believe that the blame should be placed in my lap. Many preachers have the backbone that is the consistency of a boiled noodle, and they are afraid of offending people. But I try not to be like those charlatans. I feel the need to spend some time teaching a point that many preachers are either to scared to preach (Some preachers do not teach Bible doctrine because they are are afraid of loosing financial support.) I think that other preachers may be to ignorant to loudly proclaim the WORD of GOD. Whatever the excuse is, this is the story that the Bible explains. Women and men are created by GOD with different roles, women are not men that have not yet grown a penis. GOD designed women to think differently than men. Women have this desire to be in control, but most of them do not want to be holding the package when it blows up. I call this behavior 'leading from the back' and sheep dogs lead from the back.

The modern day church system has greatly messed with the mind sets of many men and women. Today there are people that have male parts, but they have been neutered by the world and they are too afraid to make decisive decisions (meanwhile the church system says nothing). At the same time, the world has been telling women slogans like 'GOD might have designed men to be the head/leadership of the marriage...but women turn the head'. That's not a humorous phrase, instead it is a phrase that is designed to poke GOD in the eye...meanwhile the church system says little to nothing about the rebellious statements.

Genesis 3:16

(To the woman He said) *"I will greatly multiply your pain in childbirth,*

and in pain you will bring forth children;
your desire will be for your husband,
and he will rule over you."

What that means is that women want to 'lead from the back', but GOD said that idea would not pass inspection. Women have the desire to lead, but they are not designed to lead. It needs to be known that GOD created the man to be the covering (like leader). Weak minded preachers have tried to cozy up with the world. Those hypocrites are mainly interested in studying topics that can increase the strangle hold that they have on people. There should have been godly men and women that stood up with authority and declared that GOD has designed men and women and each has different functions. Please turn to **Ephesians 5**...many preachers will try to say that the Biblical model for marriage is that the husband and the wife totally love each other, well those charlatans will get whats coming to them, but what the WORD of GOD says is that the Biblical model for marriage is that the man demonstrates the behavior of CHRIST to his wife, and that the wives are supposed to submit to the Godly behavior of her husband in the same way that the true Body of CHRIST submits to the authority of CHRIST. Many preachers might be able to give advice that sounds like a good idea, but I am not concerned with a good sounding idea. Instead I want to follow what the Bible says. The divorce rate among 'christians' and the divorce rate of non-christians is almost identical. I think that allowing so called 'preachers' to take part in a marriage ceremony is almost like 'a kiss of death'. When I read Ephesians 5, I do not see the words 'wives love your husbands'. I am able to see the words 'Wives submit (yield, be respectful) to you husbands as a service to the LORD'. A lot of preachers probably got the advice 'just love each other' from the book of '2nd Opinions' (many preachers like to speak from that book).

Now back to the story of JESUS and the demoniac. As can be seen the nephilium want to wear an earth suit. The ultimate goal seems to want to posses a human suit, but if a human suit is not available then the highest living thing is the goal. Perhaps you have figured out that nephilim are the same things as aliens. I think that those nephilim spirits/aliens are trying hard to mimic GOD's creation and create a human suit...but they cant do it! The beliefs that I have at this time says that aliens are trying to 'piece together' a bunch of parts and 'make' a human. Also I think that 'the mark of the beast' is going to be presented like it is a 'upgrade'. I think that some sort of lie will be told that will cause people to think that if they will reject the system that GOD designed, then they will be able to run faster or jump higher. At that point there will be two different classifications of people, the first classification of people will be the humanoids (the ones that are part human and part nephilim/alien). The second classification of people will be the regular humans. The regular humans will not be allowed to participate in the humanoid economy, and that will cause many people to buy into that lie and they will tamper with the earth suit that GOD gave them. It is my belief that this supposed upgrade will back-fire. The supposed upgrade might claim to allow humans to run faster, jump higher, be smarter, have eyes like a hawk, be smarter, maby the 'upgrade' will tell people that they can fly or live with greater ease, but do not call GOD an old fashioned creator, because GOD knows best. Whatever the 'upgrade' claims to be, it will most likely change a persons D.N.A. I have heard people suggest that mark of the beast that is discussed in **Revelation 13:16-17**, might not only unlock a new financial system but the mark might also transform the D.N.A. of people. When the idea that the mark will change the financial system but also might create certain 'D.N.A. enhancements', then **Revelation 6:16** is referenced. Perhaps that army of people that have chosen to enhance their D.N.A. will make up the almost unstoppable army that surrounds the 'king of the north' that is talked about in **Daniel 11:40**.

I am going to try to be more clear about what I think **Revelation 12-13** teaches. A person needs to understand that the physical realm is just a shadow of the things that are taking place in the spiritual realm. The Bible teaches people to study, the Bible needs to be studied but also an attempt should be made to have a decent amount of moderate competency. Unfortunately the way that many preachers study the Bible is to just listen to the popular opinions of others and the only 'study' that is done is how fat that they, themselves, are getting. However there is a Biblical discipline called hermeneutics. Hermeneutics is how to understand the Bible.

As I have said, the way that some preachers 'seriously study' is to place their fingers into the air and try to figure out which direction the breeze is blowing. To illustrate the dangers of this type of 'study', the following example will be given. In the 1950's if a person was described as being 'gay' it meant that person was carefree and happy, but 50 years later if someone was described as 'gay' the persons sexual orientation was being questioned. If such a large change occurred in 50 years then why should people listen to preachers that disregard what was being said a couple of thousand years ago. Think about a person that was born in the 1800's, how do you think they would describe a cellular phone? In the book of Revelation, John was shown visions of things that was going to take place in the future, but I do not think he had the words to describe. To my knowledge the word 'airplane' or 'helicopter' is never used in the Bible, but that does not mean that that aircraft's are never discussed. <**Revelation 9:7-9**> I do not think that the words 'battle tank' appears in the Bible, but it seems like John was describing a battle tank that had a red, blue, and yellow flag painted on it. <**Revelation 9:17**>

The vast majority of preachers preform biblical research that would put them in the top of there class...as long as there peers were elementary school children! Many (many) churches do not even mention the nephilum, although what those unholy beings did was a big deal. The small percentage of churches that do talk about those unholy beings, they assume that GOD eliminated the problem in the Old Testament. Many of you guys need to stop listening to the convoluted logic of the money grubbers that claim to be church leaders. Its true that GOD is more than powerful enough to stomp out any problem, but GOD wants us to be strong. GOD could have made us all robots, but I guess GOD does not like the 'love' that robots produce. This is an important point because communism will only work if everybody was a robot. Communism is a very 'equal' way to deal with things, but it will not work because it will only work in a world that GOD did not design. The truth is that the benefit of being a Kingdomite is not to avoid hardship, in fact in my experience Kingdomites are perhaps more likely to experience hardship because hardship has a way of knocking off our rough edges **Ephesians 6:10-20**.

If I am understanding what **Revelation 12** is saying, in the future/ currently there is a battle being fought and the looser is going to be satan (another point that most preachers fail to mention is that 'the concept of time' only applies in this realm). As a result, satan is going to be cast to earth where the mother of the male child is (the male child is JESUS and the 'mother' of the child is the true Christians). The satan tries to persecute the mother of the child,but the woman is divinely protected for 3 1/2 years <**Revelation 12:14**>. Many preachers have invented a theology that they refer to as the pre-trib rapture, and thoes preachers speak against what the Bible teaches (**Revelation 12:14, & Revelation 13:7**). Those arrogant preachers like to inflate themselves by saying things like 'I have read the end of the book...', the problem is I think all they read was the end of the book. Anyway they missed the fact that the Bible says that part of the anti-christ system is going to attack the true Church <**Revelation 13:7**>.I do not understand exactly how but when the satan was cast down to earth then the antichrist showed up. I was trying to point out is that after the satan was cast down and before the antichrist landed on earth...I believe that between thoes two points a switch occurred. In **Revelation 12:9** the Bible talks about a purely spiritual being that does not have a body, then in **Revelation 13:1** satan's ugly twin brother shows up. In the un-holy trinity satan has claimed the role of 'father' and he does not have a body. Somehow he got a hold of a half human suit and he stuffed his twin brother in it, but anyway in 13:1 we see a nephilium (or what some people call an alien) arriving to earth and it looks very similar (but it is not identical). The satan and his brother both have seven heads and ten horns, but somehow satan's nephilim/brother figured out a way to make himself even uglier by adding 3 more crowns <please compare **Revelation 12:3** with **Revelation 13:1**>. I feel the need to correct the derelict teachings of many churches that teach that the only thing that is above earth is space, but in **Genesis 1:7** the Bible teaches that there is a quantity of water above our heads. I feel that it is important to realize that when the Bible says that the antichrist is going to "rise out of the blackness of the sea" maby what was being discussed was the 'sky sea'. While I am on the subject of incorrect teachings and end time events, some people think that miraculous works are the true sign of a person of God. **Revelation 13:13** explains that the third member of the un-holy trinity (or the third member of the three stooges), that guy is going to deceive people because he is going to be able to preform miraculous works like making fire come out of heaven. So remember if you think that someone is the greatest thing since sliced bread but what they say does not come into agreement with the Authority that is laid out in Scripture, then give that person there marching orders!

However the antichrist is going to arrogantly proclaim that he is more advanced than GOD, and it is my belief that the arrogant proclamations of the antichrist is going to be know as 'the mark of the beast'. Not only will the people that take the mark of the beast going to be taking sides against CHRIST, it is my belief that the mark of the beast will transform people into nephilium. The mark of the beast seems to be the thing that GOD hates <**Matthew 24:37**> because GOD hates people falling in love with the 'fine things' that this world has to offer <**Matthew 6:24**>.

The False Idea of Two Messiah's

As the rabbis studied scripture most prophecies concerning the Messiah seemed to fall into two categories. One of the views was that when the messiah arrived the title that would be given to him would 'mashiach ben Yosef' (messiah son of Joseph). The other view was that the title 'mashiach ben David' (messiah son of David) be placed on him.

The question was asked to Rabbi Joshua if the coming messiah would come 'with the clouds of heaven' (As in **Daniel 9:23** which depicts the Messiah coming as a victor) or if the messiah would come 'lowly riding on a donkey' (As in **Zechariah 9:9** which depicts the Messiah coming as a servant). Rabbi Joshua responded, 'if they are meritorious, he will come with the clouds of heaven; if not, lowly riding upon an ass' ~Talmud Sanh. 98A

The thought that some orthodox Jewish people had was that for some the messiah would be a suffering servant, and for others the messiah would appear as a victorious king. Then modern christianity came along and said that at the first coming of the messiah (about 4 B.C. – 30 A.D.) the world witnessed the suffering servant. However when the LORD JESUS CHRIST returns, then the world will witness the victorious king.

After some study, I have found that both views are wrong. To the orthodox Jewish view I would ask what kind of king is only able to rule over well behaved subjects? And to the traditional christian view I would say that they can only be right if what CHRIST said is ignored.

Both the orthodox Jewish view and the traditional Christianity view do not think that it is possible for a 'Servant, GOD, King' to be in one human body at the same time, but JESUS proved both of these ideas to be wrong!

John 18:36

> Jesus answered, "**My Kingdom** (GOD is the KING over the Kingdom) *is not an earthly kingdom. If it were, my followers would fight to keep me from **being handed over** (JESUS was the suffering servant) to the Jewish leaders. But my Kingdom is not of this world."*

The orthadox Jewish view and the traditional Christian view do not realize that GOD has already establish HIS Kingdom in the earthly realm. JESUS pointed out that something can be happening in the earthly realm and something entirely different could be happening in the spiritual realm.

(information source: http://jewishroots.net/library/messianic/two-messiahs-2.html)

Often, historical accounts record the actions of people that sometimes act before all of the facts are known. Such is the situation that we read about in the Bible. People actually thought that the promised MESSIAH was going to sweep in and beat up the Romans (at the time that JESUS was born the Roman government controlled the country of Israel.) Even John the Baptist shared in this line of thought. This can be seen in an account that took place while John was in prison.

Mathew 11:2-3

> *2 When John, who was in prison, heard about the deeds of the Messiah, he sent his disciples 3 to ask him, "Are you the one who is to come, or should we expect someone else?"*

John was confused, on the one hand he knew that JESUS was sent by GOD but on the other hand he had been put in prison because he was telling people about how the KING had arrived. John's confusion was not an isolated event. After JESUS had went to the cross, had been buried, and then broke out of the grave, JESUS spent some time doing what HE thought needed to be done. Then came the day when HE was going to make like a tree and leaf out of here. That day is recorded in the book of Acts.

Acts 1:6-8

> *6 So when they had come together, they asked Him, "Lord, will You at this time restore the kingdom to Israel?" 7 He said to them, "It is not for you to know the times or the dates, which the Father has fixed by His own authority. 8 But* (Stop asking when is GOD going to fix things) *you shall receive power when the Holy Spirit comes upon you. And you shall be My witnesses in Jerusalem, and in all Judea and Samaria, and to the ends of the earth."*

JESUS's disciples still did not quite understand that they were looking at The KING that was interested in expanding HIS Kingdom, however the territory that JESUS was interested in is located inside of people. The disciples knew that JESUS was the Anointed Messiah that the prophecies were about. However what the rabbi's were teaching proved to be incorrect, because they knew that the KING had suffered and laid down HIS life. In there minds the KING had already suffered but it was also obvious that Israel had not yet been restored, so the only logical question was 'When was the KING going to put Israel back on top?'

The mindset of the Jewish Rabbi's, and the mindset of many modern day preachers is similar. Both groups of individuals assume that the KING has already begun to establish HIS Kingdom inside of the earthly realm. But the Kingdom of GOD is designed to function like an ant colony. The ant colony only spends a percentage of its time working where they can be seen. When the work of the ant colony cannot be seen that does not mean that the ant colony is no longer functioning. In Acts 1 the disciples incorrectly assumed two things. The first incorrect thought that the disciples had was that they assumed that 100% of the Kingdom was going to be fully viable to their physical eyes. The second misconception that the disciples had was that they believed that JESUS was going to do all of the work.

What I am trying to establish is the fact that many early followers of CHRIST were confused about what JESUS was the KING of. This confusion was not resolved (for some) by the death, burial, and resurrection of CHRIST. Some people did not understand what the KING was doing on earth, and since the KING is quite capable of carrying out HIS will...then what did the KING want mankind to do? It is impossible for any of us to 'create change' without the power that GOD The HOLY SPIRIT gives. So any 'church' or organization that claims to be working towards change without the aid of GOD The HOLY SPIRIT, is not using a legitimate means. In the spiritual realm that is an illegal operation. Lets look at what is going on, the KING said that we would receive enough power to (for example) move a rock...the power would arrive after we ate the ham sandwich. Today unscrupulous men and women that are claiming that the rock can be moved even if the ham sandwich is not eaten. Ladies and gentlemen if the results could be achieved another way, then why would have the KING wasted HIS breath. Men and women with slick ears have tried to stand up and preach that GOD The HOLY SPIRIT is no longer relevant. The only word that I know to label what those people are saying is 'Blasphemy' **Mark 3:27-29**.

I am about to point out a teaching of JESUS that probably 98-99% of churches do not teach. In fact some churches demonstrate how inept they are by actually claiming that GOD the HOLY SPIRIT is no longer available for the believer today, and they are certain that GOD the HOLY SPIRIT has not given them any power. The situation becomes even more painfully humorous when those pathetic individuals begin to chant to the 'god' that they serve and they ask it to send them revival.

After an honest reading of the WORDS that JESUS spoke in **Acts 1:6-8**, it is quite clear that denominations that claim such things are working hard to fulfill something but they can not be laboring for The KINGDOM of GOD.

(Checkmate)

GOD The HOLY SPIRIT
My Best Friend!

Let's look at the last thing that JESUS said before HE left planet earth.

Acts 1:4^b-5

> **Jesus:** 4^b *This is what you heard Me teach— 5 just like John (the baptist) ritually cleansed people with water through baptism, so you will be washed with the Holy Spirit very soon.*

In this passage JESUS clearly spells out that John the baptist acted like a reflection. John's life was a model, it can be said that his life was like a shadow. The reflection that was seen through the life of John pointed to the final product. Just like -The shadow- (which was John) 'dipped' people into water, -The real deal- (which was JESUS) 'dipped' people into GOD the HOLY SPIRIT. **Matthew 3:3** (John the baptist was the forerunner of CHRIST. The job of John was to prepare people to follow JESUS.)

Acts 1:6

> **Location:** *When they (JESUS and the disciples) had gathered just outside Jerusalem at the Mount of Olives, they (The disciples) asked Jesus,*

Disciples: _Is now the time_, Lord—the time _when You will reestablish Your kingdom_ in our land of Israel?

The disciples were still under the impression that JESUS was an earthly KING. As an earthly 'king' the disciples were ready for JESUS to kick the Roman army out of Israel. (Since the time that GOD had cursed the family line of jechonias the nation of Israel had little to no leadership. Understanding the leadership vacuum that existed in Israel is very important!) Israel desperately wanted a king that could unite troops, and lead in military campaigns. The country had gone without much leadership for the past few hundred years. At that time Israel was everyone's punching bag, so they were waiting for a king. But they did not share the same vision of the Kingdom of GOD (The book of Matthew was written with the Jewish people in mind, and the Jewish people do not want to take the LORD's NAME in vain... so instead of saying the Kingdom of GOD, the book of Matthew says The Kingdom of Heaven.) While I am on that subject I will mention that the church system has a messed up view of many things. Another of the messed up views that the church system tries to pawn off on people is their misunderstanding of Heaven. The church system teaches that people need to accept the message of CHRIST so that the person can go to Heaven when they die? **Acts 2:34** teaches us that king David is not in Heaven, and in **John 3:13** JESUS said _"No one has ascended into heaven, but He who descended from heaven: the Son of Man."_ So, there is that!

When JESUS said that HE was the KING of the Jews (or the KING of the true Christians (not just Jewish people), **Romans 11:11-24** many people thought that JESUS had come to earth so that HE might establish The Kingdom of GOD in the Middle East. That's why Herod wanted to kill baby JESUS. Herod was a puppet king that the Roman Empire had installed, and his 'kingdom' was in the middle east. When

Herod heard that the KING had been born in Israel then Herod was just trying to stomp out a rebellion before the rebellion started when he tried to kill the baby KING.

So **Acts 1:6** the disciples were just asking when GOD The FATHER had chosen for JESUS to establish The Kingdom of GOD in the country of Israel. Today the question might seem a little weird, but back then GOD had always used the nation of Israel to teach the world about GOD. (GOD seems to like to establish a model.) Just like GOD used John the baptist to teach people that 'We need GOD to wash over us' (like water baptism) and then JESUS taught people that 'GOD's endgame' was for ordinary people to help establish the Kingdom of GOD. Just like water baptism is an signal that the person has surrendered their lives and claimed that in and of themselves those people do not know the correct way to live, being baptized with The SPIRIT of GOD is a representation that physical humans do not understand how to help build The Kingdom of GOD. JESUS was referring to this teaching in **John 3:5** when HE said:

John 3:5

> Jesus answered, "Truly, truly I say to you, <u>unless</u> a man is <u>born of water</u> and <u>the Spirit, he cannot enter the king-dom of God</u>.

I have heard idiotic morons that claim to be ministers say stupid things like 'I believe that GOD The HOLY SPIRIT stopped personally interacting with believers'. Then those chowder heads have the nerve to ask their 'god' to please send revival to there churches. Why would GOD want to wast HIS time and resuscitate insubordinate institutions like that? People that believe in such malarkey should hang a sign over the doors that says '**Ichabod'** (**1 Samuel 4:21**). I am not saying that there are small pockets of dumbcoffs that actually think that 'they' can help build the Kingdom of GOD without the infilling of GOD The HOLY SPIRIT, instead I am telling you that major 'church' denominations have bought into the crap teaching that their own beliefs are more important than what the KING said. They are about as ridiculous as a blind person trying to go bird watching. (Although all people can enjoy nature, not every person enjoys the great outdoors for the same reason.)

Acts 1:7

> **JESUS:** *The Father, on His own authority, has determined the ages and epochs of history, but you have not been given this knowledge.*

In other words JESUS told the diciples that the way that the question was worded implied that for The Kingdom of GOD to appear GOD The FATHER needed to 'elevate' JESUS. After JESUS explained that what was being asked was not the business of the diciples, next Jesus explained the information that the guys wanted. Often the questions that people asked JESUS were not in the correct ballpark. Of course because JESUS is GOD, JESUS not only heard the misguided question, but JESUS also knew with certainty how to give the answer that was needed. So the topic of the question that was being asked was 'how is GOD going to establish The Kingdom of GOD on this earth'? But the disciples presumed that they were going to be bystanders, but they were wrong. In effect JESUS said 'you guys need to stop thinking about how GOD The FATHER is going to use The SON to bring restoration to the world, because GOD The HOLY SPIRIT is going to empower people to help build The Kingdom.

GOD has chosen to establish HIS Kingdom in sections. The first section (the one that I am going to be talking about anyway) was built by JESUS, and HE was 100% GOD but HE was also 100% man. Even though JESUS was a flesh and blood human being that walked on the face of this earth HE was also 100% GOD and HE made a choice to not establish HIS Kingdom in the same dimension that earth exists in. JESUS was part of the first 'wave' of Kingdom builders but HE was also the blueprint of Kingdom workers. Even though we are human beings when GOD The HOLY SPIRIT *comes on* (or in-fills us) then we are able to exist in the earthly realm but we can work at 'Kingdom builders Inc.'

Acts 1:8

> **JESUS:** *Here's the knowledge you need: you will receive power when the Holy Spirit comes on you. And you will be My witnesses, first here in Jerusalem, then beyond to Judea and Samaria, and finally to the farthest places on earth.*

JESUS had already explained that their KING was not abandoning them so that they would be orphans, rather GOD the SON and GOD The HOLY SPIRIT were sort of 'tag-teaming' the earth. JESUS had already explained that HE needed to go and it was to our benefit that GOD the SON left (earth) because then GOD The HOLY SPIRIT would be able to 'infuse' the lives of believers.

John 16:7

> *"...I tell you the truth, it is to your advantage that I go away* (from earth)*; for if I do not go away, the Helper* (GOD The HOLY SPIRIT) *will not come to you; but if I go, I will send Him to you.*

You might be wondering why the KING would rely on a guy like me to help build HIS Kingdom. I have wondered that myself, because if GOD has a 'B' team I am surly on it. And I do not feel like I am captain of the 'B' team, sometimes I feel that I am a starting play for the position of 'left bench'.

But it does not matter how I or any other human feels. Instead it is my job to figure out what the KING said and then do it! And the KING gave us all a commission to prepare soil. Just like the soil must be prepared to build any sort of building, the KING will not build on soil that has been uncultivated. But the KING is not interested in territory that can be found on a map. The Kingdom of GOD will be built and expanded on territory that is inside the souls of mankind!

Welcome to the Edges of the Field!

I know of a situation where thieves were targeting religious institutions. Only items that could be quickly converted into cash money were stolen. Because small items were taken it could probably be assumed that the thieves were only interested in a quick profit. I took the liberty of assuming that the thieves needed money to buy food.

While the thieves were clearly in the wrong, I was able to see the irony in the situation. Institutions that were designed to help humanity out of a 'tight spot' those institutions were in a situation where they were forcing needy individuals to have to break down doors so that the needs could be met. The religious institutions were only 'helping' individuals at certain times. I certainly believe in the value of robust locks and secure doors, and churches and religious institutions have every right to secure their establishments, however I could not help but see the irony in a thief having to break-in to a place just to receive assistance.

The simple truth is that many 'religious institutions' are following a counterfeit game plan. I want to talk about the counterfeit game plan...its called communism. The communist game plan is an approach that attempts to treat individuals equally. That game plan would be a very logical approach to distributing aid except human beings are not robots. Humanity is flawed, and communism teaches people that it is a good idea to see which person can get the greatest amount of 'help' while doing the least amount of work. The Bible clearly explains to us that communism does not even start out on the correct foot. The communist plan works perfectly when dealing with robots.

Ecclesiastics 4:4

> Then I observed that most <u>people are motivated to success because they envy</u> their neighbors....

But humans are not machines, in fact sometimes I respond differently even though the stimuli is the same. If one person does not always respond the same way, then why do people expect a 'one size fits all' communist system to meet people's needs. Comparisons can be made between communism and the American school system, both systems might work well for a small number of people but in the long run neither of the two systems are sustainable.

Of course many religious institutions adopt a system of distributing aid that is linked to mammon **(Matthew 6:24)**, and when pressure is applied they fold up like a cheap card table. But maby you are wondering why many would adopt such a 'looser' policy to distribute aid. The answer is because power corrupts people.

<u>Absolute power corrupts absolutely</u> - -John Emerich Edward Dalberg
Acton, 1887

If you do not believe John or myself, then go to a school room and give a kid a whistle. Tell him that he is in charge of making sure everyone stands in a line, and watch how the kid will only speak with authority at the proper time. It is true that not all social programs are under the direction of power hungry individual, but unfortunately much 'leadership' is a power-grab. Sometimes 'authority' is only exercised when the group benefits, but many times the job only gets done when the ego of the leadership is stroked. That is why Americas founding fathers created more than one government office. When any leader is given a 'leadership hat' that is too big, then the leaders head tends to enlarge itself. Two kinds of humans exist, #1 Some people are just tyrants and #2 The rest of the people are tyrants in the making. I like to think that I am a nice guy but if you give me a whistle, I might blow it so hard that the 'whistle pea' disintegrates. Its just our nature, we humans are a miserable bunch.

Jeremiah 17:9

> *The heart is deceitful above all things and beyond cure.*
> *Who can understand it?*

So I started to think about how GOD instructed Kingdomites to deal with the situation of human need, because it is not the best idea to allow humans to solve the problems. Its true that only GOD is able to handle power and not become corrupt, but also if a society of people dedicated their life savings in an effort to end poverty then that society would just get sucked dry. Is it possible that GOD directed Kingdomites to fully rely on GOD to do all of the heavy lifting?

Leviticus 23:22

> *"'When you reap the harvest of your land, do not reap*
> *to the very edges of your field or gather the gleanings of*
> *your harvest. Leave them for the poor and for the foreign-*
> *er residing among you. I am the LORD your God.'"*

'The edges of the field' is not designed like a food bank or a soup kitchen. GOD designed the edges of the field to capitalize on the free market system. Unlike the communistic model that says 'everybody should share', the free market system places charity out of the control of humans. When times were lean, I have collected a few apples off of a tree and had myself a snack. Make no mistake...GOD placed the apples on that tree, and the apples were left there because of the free market society.

I think that it would be nice if some people planted some fruit/nut trees/plants at the edges of their properties. Of course the tree would need to be marked as a 'charity tree', this would be to avoid confusion. Many needy people are not wanting to steal a persons food, so people should mark the sections that are to produce 'charity food' and which sections are intended to be for 'private use'. Take GOD up on HIS offer and allow HIM to provide for the needy.

I want to take a brief moment and talk about communism. The idea that is behind communism is an extremely benevolent idea, but as we have discussed no human exists that can oversee such a system. I have not stated the obvious, because it almost makes me cringe...but I will, 'most people hate GOD' and they would rather drowned than ask GOD to float a life preserver their way. But there is one more 'force' that I believe is going to try to implement communism. And that 'force' will be able to keep the system 'a float' for a while (Remember that communism will work,until you spend everyone elses money...then it will fail..horibly.) This 'force' will be know as the antichrist system. **Revelation 13:15-17**

Some people disengage their brains when it comes to charity. Its like when ever there is a problem suddenly everybody turns into 'Daddy Warbucks'. Its crazy how many people think that every problem can be solved with 'more money, more money, and if that does not fix things then the situation must require more money'.

There are three main issues that need to be honestly addressed if we hope to get a handle on poverty:

- Sometimes poverty is a mindset, not everyone is poor because they are victims of circumstance. There are certain groups of people that think that society needs to change. I hate how this world operates, but I realize that some times protocol needs to be followed or else things will not happen. Its like if I begin to dial a 10 digit phone number, but I forget the last 2 digits of the number then I have no right to be offended when the phone company fails to connect me. Somethings exist where a person needs to follow the rules very closely. Maby a small percentage of people that are non conformists are 'warriors for justice', but some people are just waiting for all the broken glass that they have collected to be worth millions of dollars. Thats why a sports star can have a bank account of a couple of million dollars when they retire, but in a couple of years they end up with no money. Its like a recipe that a person needs to follow. It is easy to preform the passive action of throwing money at the poverty monster, but sometimes the persons mindset needs to change. Rather than trying to take wealth from the people 'the have' and giving it to the 'have nots' (which is a redistribution of the wealth), I think that it would be nice if some people volunteered to teach a class on financial education. Sometimes the donations that people give they reinforce the belief that success is handed out. Instead of helping to motivate poor people to become more successful, sometimes giving people things only keeps people trapped in the vicious cycle of stinking thinking.

- People need to develop some discernment. This will come as a shock to some people but there is a breed of individuals that will hold there hands out for help and they might be in better financial shape than what you think. I am defiantly not trying to say that every person that claims to have a need is a phony, because some people just need help getting back on there feet. But some people actually lie about how much need they have, and some people will intentionally enter into situations just so they can receive more help. So the people that have some ability to give a financial contribution need to ask GOD to give them discernment, because sometimes thoes people are being played...like a fiddle!

• Not all help should be the same. I call the two categories the 'now need' and the 'long term need'. Now needs can be met with a can of beans, or a bowl of soup and a warm bed. It is important to address a persons now needs, but now needs are often like surface level cuts. In my estimation much attention has been given to people that have now needs. Long term need are not always easy to help solve, which would explain why so few organizations are dedicated to help solve the problems. A saying that I heard does a good job at defining the two needs, the saying goes like this *'for every 1,000 axes chopping away at the tree of evil only one ax is laid to the root'*. Many people will grab an ax and work to chop off a branch of the 'tree of need', but not many people realize that if the root is chopped up then the tree withers. The needy person might be living in such a way that leads to poverty, so some sort of training/educational material needs to be taught. What I am trying to say is that dealing with 'now needs' are important, but treating all problems as if they were now needs can be a little self defeating.

I tried to point out The Kingdom of GOD is a Kingdom of LOVE (because GOD is LOVE) **1 John 4:7-21**). It is important to realize that humans did not create LOVE, rather LOVE created humans. Something that separates 'Christianity' from other religions is the fact that GOD sent Pure LOVE to the world with the purpose of teaching people to act like LOVE acts. That is why I have been using the term 'Kingdomite', or one who models the behavior of the KING. The way that most people live is extremely selfish, As far as they are concerned, they are #1. A favorite past time that many people enjoy is looking out for number one. LOVE is anti-selfishness and incorporating Love would mean that many people could no longer enjoy their past time. Instead of actually modifying their behavior, many people want to appease there conscience and simply pay lip service to The KING. I think that many people like the idea of Love, because they do not want to be known as a selfish person. Although they like the idea of Love the concept goes against the favorite past time. The solution that many people come up with is they donate a couple of dollars and call it a day.

I think that a proper conversation about The Kingdom of GOD/LOVE should provide some direction about how Kingdomites should conduct themselves. Do not think that it is wrong to have money. While on earth JESUS spent a good amount of time teaching people how they should deal with material possessions. GOD blesses us so that we can bless others. So get your head out of the sand and stop assuming that it is wrong for you to have stuff. What is wrong is for people to have stuff and do nothing about the sufferings of there neighbors. I do not think that some people have a clue about what the purpose of life is. **Spoiler Alert** I am about to let the cat out of the bag:

Genesis 1:28

> And God blessed them. And God said to them, "Be fruitful and multiply and <u>fill the earth and subdue it</u>, and <u>have dominion over</u> the fish of the sea and <u>over</u> the birds of the heavens and <u>over</u> every living thing that moves on the earth."

Question: Why does GOD care if we have means to do things? **Answer:** (The daily double...that was a joke!) The real reason why GOD cares if you have the means to do anything is so a person can take dominion over _____.

Pretend that a food pantry receives most of its funding from working families. This food pantry is able to provide assistance to 100 families per month. One day the economy goes south and the food pantry receives 25% less support, as a result the food pantry is only able to provide 75 meals. So when the food pantry is unable to help a lot of people, that is the time that a greater number of folks need assistance. I guess that a couple of different lessons can be drawn from the example that we just looked at. However a lesson that I would like for people to understand is that most people's idea of charity is to 'give themselves poor', and that is only a good plan until people start running out of money. Communism is like that, 'its a good idea and it works...until the other guy runs out of money, at that point things are about as humorous as trying to crawl out of a hole that is nine feet deep and only having two ladders that are 4 feet tall each.

The idea behind the edges of the field is simple. Let GOD handle the poor people, and just plant a fruit tree. GOD is tasked with taking care of the tree, and HE is the ONE that will put food on the tree. If it was an entirely human endeavor all of the food would be placed at the top of the tree, and the government would require a big piece of fruit for it's self. The edges of the field might seem like a passive attitude to have, but it requires me to admit that the job is to big for me. I am able to claim that if a person decides to plant an apple tree and adopts the edges of the field strategy then the apple tree should be able to produce a greater amount of food than what could be bought if the apple tree was not purchased. So the edges of the field strategy is much more economical. Under normal conditions the trees will produce fruit year after year, GOD will water the tree and give the tree sunlight.

If mankind was in charge of designing the fruit tree then the edges of the field would be a terrible idea! But the idea is certain to succeed because human intervention would be kept to a minimal amount. Generaly speaking the intervention of human beings is a plan that ends in disaster. "That government the governs least, governs best" --Henry David Thoreau. (Human beings are fundamentally selfish.)

Jeremiah 17:9

> The heart is deceitful above all things, and it is extremely sick; Who can understand it fully and know its secret motives?

It is easy to see that mankind is not nearly as smart as he thinks that he is. Although the mouth of mankind might say that they want to help people, it is important for us to remember that the hearts of mankind is deceitful. Like a Venus flytrap does not try to attract insects towards it by producing vinegar, instead sweet smelling nectar is produced to attract insects. I think that most people would be happy to help someone out for the low cost of $19.95, but if you act now they will double the offer and throw the smile in for free (Shipping and handling is not included.)

Lets think about deceit for a moment. The true motives of the heart are about as lovely as a pig that is wearing a pearl necklace. No matter how dressed up and fancy the pig is made out to be the fact remains that it is still a pig. The Bible tells us that the true motives of the human heart is a bigger whopper than an evening gown on a pig!

The truth is that mankind can never eradicate poverty by simply giving their money away, that is called self sabotage. It does not matter how quickly your shovel moves or how deep of a hole that you dig, humanity can not dig itself out of a hole! The majority of people think that if they "spread the wealth around then poverty will be no more", but that is a communistic idea. The only thing that that communism is able to do is make everyone equally poor. Communism is the increasingly awful idea that a bunch of guys that had fallen into a hole came up with. They could not agree which side of the hole they should climb out of, so they took the biggest ladder and cut it into pieces so that everyone can have the same size of step stool.

As It says in:
Ecclesiastics 4:4

> *'I saw that all toil and every skillful work come from one man's envy of another.'*

Most work that has ever been done on this earth, and most of work that will ever be done on this earth is done because person 'A' wants to some how better themselves. In physics, a force is said to do work if, when acting, there is a movement of the point of application in the direction of the force. Basically, if I throw a baseball towards a batter, and the batter decides that he likes the direction that the ball is traveling then there is no need for any more work to be done. However, if I throw a baseball towards a batter, and the batter decides that he does not like the direction that the ball is traveling then he must preform work (or a force) and the amount of work that is done by the batter will determine the speed (and distance) that the baseball travels. Many people want to pretend that life is like a game of 'cosmic' baseball. They send the batter to the plate without a bat and reassure the person to 'use the schwartz'.

All of the people that need a helping hand can be fit into two categories.

- The first category would contain the people that have a temporary need. An example of a temporary need would be someone falling and breaking their leg. More than likely that person is not going to be able to work as much for a short time and they will benefit from a food basket. (And I will say that I am glad that temporary assistance is available.)

- The second category would contain the people that have a long term need. An example of a person that has a long term need is the guy that lives in a community where a large percentage of workers were all laid off. A bag full of groceries would probably still be appreciated in that situation, but it would be like putting a bandage on a gunshot wound.

I do not want people to think that I am trying to discourage people from making donations to food banks and soup kitchens. But I will explain why 'poverty' can not be solved by only focusing on people that have temporary needs. The problem is that many people do not understand 'basic finances'. Most people think that the correct way to solve problems is to throw money at the problem. Basic logic says that if 'Person A' has $100 and 'Person B' has $0 then the problem can be solved by 'redistributing the wealth'. Whenever terms like 're-distribute the wealth' are used, an economic system know as communism is being discussed. Communism works great...until you run out of other peoples money, then it fails...horrifyingly. But as long as other people have money then the communistic system works well! Notice that a communistic hand out more than likely begins a death spiral. A death spiral is not always the case of a free handout, but free stuff has a tendency to teach the majority of people that they do not need a baseball bat in order to change the direction of the baseball.

I want to belabor this point. I support the free market (lazifare economics), not just because I think that it is a better system than communism. But the main reason why people should support free market capitalism is because they do not want to put to much hope in a ticking time bomb! Communism might seem like a 'merry-go-round' type of joy ride but that is because people have not yet arrived at the end of the death spiral. Capitalism might sounds like it is something that only a greedy person would like to be apart of, but many people confuse 'capitalism' with its illegitimate cousin that is named 'crony capitalism'. Real Capitalism is just a system that allows people to receive awards based off of how much effort they put into the job, but there is an almost secrete bonus to having a Capitalistic system and that is the more effort the entire community exerts then the more my life is enriched. The bonus of Capitalism is why people want to live in a established community. In true Capitalism death spirals are non existant. Instead of a 'death spiral', the community sometimes creates an 'updraft'. True Capitalism allows people to fail if they make business decisions that are unwise, however crony capitalism (which is borderline communism) say certain institutions are to big to fail, therefore money needs to be taken from the responsible businesses and given to support those who make poor decisions.

A very simple definition of communism is 'share' (which sounds like a very good idea) until a person realizes that 'share' means 'share the dollars, but it also means share the debt'. Which is a great idea (if you are a slacker). What self respecting slacker would not be happy share a bank account with a responsible person and then spend half of the money in the bank account. The word 'share' almost produces an expectation that everyone will springboard off of the success of the next guy. But what communism does is it takes away a persons incentive to do better. 'Share' might sound like a good idea, but 'share' is just what they call 'the race to the bottom'. If I am going to receive the same reward regardless if I work hard and manufacture 5 cars, or if I take it easy and produce 4 cars then why should I mound up grief for myself. I will produce the minimal amount of effort and as a result I will gain all of the benefits. The only thing that I do not want is someone to work less than me, because then a new low standard is established. Its like the game of limbo, 'lets see how low he can go'. Does this sound like the bail outs and money printing that is done by the federal reserve bank? It should sound familiar, and make no mistake each time the fed decides to 'reward' failing institutions that is called 'crony capitalism'. Every time a Crony capitalistic idea is put into place, then one more crack appears in the retaining wall.

The very simple definition for capitalism is 'healthy competition'. When the markets allow workers to compete then the workers produce better products, because Capitalism is a race to the top. So Capitalism and communism/crony capitalism are both races/competitions. One race is to the top and the other race is to the bottom! As it says:

Ecclesiastes 4:4

> I have seen that <u>every labor</u> and <u>every skill</u> in work comes from (or is produced from) <u>man's rivalry</u> with his neighbor....

So it is counter productive to expect to end poverty by collecting donations from the 'rich' and giving them to the 'poor'. Such acts of charity does well at solving emergency situations (and such aid is greatly appreciated because some needs are emergency situations -or now needs). The reason why the 'Robin Hood model', of steal from the rich and give it to the poor, only works to solve emergency situations is because the Robin Hood model removes competition/rivalry from life. The Robin Hood model is the definition of communism and it might sound like a wonderful system...but morality can not be legislated. Recently I read a news article about a talk show host who's 'company slogan' is to just be kind to others. The headline of the article caught my eye because I already knew that such a policy would end in disaster. Most people assume that humanity is filled with good natured individuals, but the Bible teaches otherwise.

Jeremiah 17:9

> The human <u>heart is the most deceitful</u> of all things, and <u>desperately wicked</u>. Who really knows how bad it is?

The devious nature of the human heart also points to the Gospel of The Kingdom of GOD. The word gospel means 'good news', and the anticipation of The Kingdom of GOD is in a category by itself. Human suffering and poverty will continue to be a part of life until The Kingdom of GOD comes. Its a popular thought that the Bible is simply a rule book and society will be better off if humanity follows it. To a large extent people should follow the teachings that are found in the Bible, but 'salvation' is not just an agreement to follow the teachings of the Bible. The act of dedicating your life to GOD is a dual experience. The first circumstance that occurs during salvation is that GOD preforms 'heart surgery'. In most surgical procedures that a medical professional preforms, the 'patient' is given a list of precautions/things that should be done and things that should not be done. Kingdomites are just a group of people that have received heart surgery and they are following (to the best of their abilities) the list of precautions (The Bible).

A group of people exists that think that if they follow the list of precautions (The Bible), that will lead to heart surgery. This group of people assume that they are able to improve on the heart surgeons (GOD) work, thoes people are fake kingdomites or 'cino's (christians in name only). As JESUS said in the 13th chapter of the book of John.

John 13:34-35

> *34 "A new commandment I give to you, that you <u>love</u>*
> *<u>one another, even as I have loved you</u>, that you also love*
> *one another. 35 <u>By this all men will know that you are</u>*
> *<u>My disciples</u>, if you have love for one another."*

There you have it, it does not matter how many Biblical precautions that a person follows. Without true Biblical LOVE being present in a persons life a person is just fooling themselves into thinking that they have had heart surgery.

What am I saying, well simply put mankind is not smart enough to create a set of rules that will balance the scales of injustice. There has only been one set of rules that has been able to guide mankind through the complex maze of human emotion...do you want me to list the set of rules, because the rules are very simple to understand. **'Love GOD and Love mankind'**.

Matthew 22:36-40

> *36 "Teacher, which is the greatest commandment in the*
> *law?"*
> *37 Jesus said to him, " 'You shall <u>love the Lord your God</u>*
> *with all your heart, and with all your soul, and with all*
> *your mind.' 38 This is the first and great commandment.*
> *39 And the second is like it: 'You shall <u>love your neighbor</u>*
> *as yourself.' 40 On these two commandments hang all*
> *the Law and the Prophets."*

I think that it is amazing how every aspect of human is designed to modeled after the character of GOD. Membership is straight forward 'if a person acts like the KING then they are in, if a person does not act like the KING then they are out'.

Many people do not even try to understand LOVE/GOD/ The KING. So let me talk about Love for a bit. The word LOVE is a noun and it is a verb (LOVE is the name of The KING, but also it is the characteristic that should be what Kingdomites do). The Bible tells us that GOD is LOVE (*1 John 4:8*). So when I tell someone that I Love them, I am telling them that I am going to try to interact with them the same way that GOD interacts with them.

I am just going to rip the bandage off, the overwhelming majority of folks do not Love, they do not try to act like LOVE, and how could they because they do not even want to know anything about LOVE.

I am by no means trying to stand up on behalf of thoes Loveless swine, but I want it to be known that the majority of thoes people try to follow the 'rules' of GOD/LOVE they just do not like how GOD/LOVE teaches to navigate through human desire. The problem is that most people are to selfish. So they trust \the kingdom of mammon to solve there dilemma. I think that the majority of people are ready to scream 'bloody murder' if they are not treated in a Biblicaly correct manner The problem that most people have with The Kingdom of GOD is that they are not the king.

Matthew

> *24 Then Jesus said to His disciples, "If anyone wishes to follow Me* [as My disciple], *he must deny himself* [set aside selfish interests], *and take up his cross* [expressing a willingness to endure whatever may come] *and follow Me* [believing in Me, conforming to My example in living and, if need be, suffering or perhaps dying because of faith in Me]. *25 For whoever wishes to save his life [in this world] will* [eventually] *lose it* [through death], *but whoever loses his life* [in this world] *for My sake will find it* [that is, life with Me for all eternity]. *26 For what will*

it profit a man if he gains the whole world [wealth, fame, success], but forfeits his soul? Or what will a man give in exchange for his soul?

The rules of the Kingdom of GOD says that **Kingdomites must be willing to swallow their pride and give the more honorable position to someone else**. Ironically, the definition of Love (as a verb), is the same as 'anti selfishness'. Most people do not want to be a member in The Kingdom of GOD because they like being selfish. However the kingdom of **mammon states that charity can be whatever you want it to be**. Oddly enough most people think that because they are charitable people, they should receive some sort of membership in The Kingdom of LOVE. Thoes people think that because they demonstrate some of the characteristics of love, by extension they are 'part love'. Using that logic S.C.U.B.A divers must be part fish, because they swim and breathe under water. **Prestige and self preservation are the most noble quests in the lives of non-Kingdomites**, it is possible for some human hearts to only give to others when it somehow benefits themselves.

Philippians 2:3-11

> *3 Do nothing from selfishness or empty conceit, but with humility of mind regard one another as more important than yourselves; 4 do not merely look out for your own personal interests, but also for the interests of others. 5 Have this attitude in yourselves which was also in Christ Jesus, 6 who, although He existed in the form of God, did not regard equality with God a thing to be grasped, 7 but emptied Himself, taking the form of a bond-servant, and being made in the likeness of men. 8 Being found in appearance as a man, He humbled Himself by becoming obedient to the point of death, even death on a cross. 9*

For this reason also, God highly exalted Him, and be-
stowed on Him the name which is above every name, 10
so that at the name of Jesus every knee will bow, of those
who are in heaven and on earth and under the earth,
11 and that every tongue will confess that Jesus Christ is
Lord, to the glory of God the Father.

Communism and socialism are not designed to be bad programs. On the contrary thoes programs are the shining brainchil-
dren of the kingdom of mammon (I already tried to explain that
most people want to show 'love' to mankind its just that they hate
the fact that GOD/LOVE wants them to stop being selfish (its kind
of like someone wanting to play chess without a king.) Communism
and socialism are honorable programs but they will not work because human beings are not robots. Communism is sort of like being a part of a Mexican standoff, because the entire program was
doomed before it started. Communism would work perfectly if only
human beings were not born with a desire to be selfish. The entire
system is a race to the bottom...like the game of limbo "how low
can you go"!

The Robin Hood model of feeding the poor will only work as
long as other people do not run out of money. But as for the edges of
the field, the concept works because mankind is not trying to control
things (that is also why the free market/capitalism works).

The one exception that I see where human intervention might
be helpful (in the edges of the field) is that a hungry person might
not realize that the apples are free. Some sort of indicating sign
would be helpful, otherwise the needy person is left to there own
devices. One time when I was in need of some food aide I walked
past an apple tree. If I remember correctly the tree was in the yard
of a vacant house. After I was certain that I was not stealing from

other, I took some apples (I figured that if I did not put the apples in my belly then they would probably just fall to the ground and rot.) But I probably would have been more at ease if someone had put up a sign!

Christian Means 'CHRIST Like'

Acts 11:26

...and the disciples were first called Christians in Antioch.

Satire is one of the forms of humor that I enjoy. Although several examples of satire exist the basics of this type of humor is to use sarcasm, ridicule, or irony to prove a point. Satire is used to show foolishness or vice in humans, organizations, or even governments.

Most likely the citizens of the city of Antioch, saw the mannerisms of the disciples and were able to understand that they were looking at people that closely mimicked the behavior of CHRIST. The word 'Christian' comes from the Greek word *christianos*, meaning 'little CHRIST'. The accusers of Jesus's disciples used the term "Christian" as an insult. The word 'christian' is actually a title that was used to classify someones behavior. What was meant to be a jeer became a badge of honor for billions of people. So an ironic jeer, that turned into a badge of honor is like double irony. But how many churches handle the double irony is ironic, because today some churches do not even attempt to study the life of CHRIST. As a result, the church has produced many individuals that claim to be christians but their lives do not even remotely resemble the life of CHRIST. So in a dramatic turn of events the non CHRIST like christians have double crossed the Antiochian hecklers.

Basicly, that is strike #2! Strike #1 was the huge disapointment of the modern day 'church system'. When JESUS said that the truth that HE is the CHRIST/awaited Messiah was going to form the foundation of the counsel that initiates change (ekklesia), and the institutional church said 'hey we think that JESUS wanted people that enjoyed sitting in nice buildings'. So the 'church system' is a pretty big disappointment. But to add insult to injury, the majority of 'church goers' are claiming a lie.

Not only are these C.I.N.O's (Christians in name only) a huge source of irony, but it is my opinion that cino's have become a stench to millions of individuals. It's unfortunate that to the untrained eye cino's appear nearly identical to real followers of CHRIST...but I want to encourage people everywhere to examine the amount of Love that a person shows. True believers in CHRIST are human and we mess up, but real Christians try to show LOVE. In my experience cino's will say that they love you...until you cross that line...then the cinos will do their best to destroy your life (then the twisted little perverts try to explain to people that if 'you' come to 'jesus' then the hell in your life will disappear. I think that it would be easier for ceno's to tell people 'I am a wolf in sheep's clothing and if you cross me then I will make your life a living hell...until you do what I say'. So I am sure that at times my own actions have not demonstrated Love, but I feel confident that I try to correct my mistakes, and replace negative interactions with Love. Which by the way none of us would even know how to Love unless GOD had sent HIS SON to earth to demonstrate how to live a lifestyle of LOVE **1 John 1:9**.

As a side note, I want to explain that what many cino's refer to as christianity is nothing more than witchcraft/wiccan spells.

It is ironic that the hierarchy that exists within the church has allowed the world to define love. I am not convinced that most church goers understand that GOD is LOVE (1 John 4:7-21). Many people think that Love is an emotion, and in one sense it is. But LOVE is also used to describe the personality of GOD. The answer to "Why does the church system think that humans, that do not even seek to understand who GOD is, should be able to define 'love'"...that answers is up for grabs. I think that the reason is one of two issues, either the church system does not know that the Bible tells us that GOD is LOVE or maby they understand that GOD is LOVE but they are too afraid to explain that to people! But I will make it clear, **the love that a non-christian have, is not the same Love that Christians should be demonstrating!**

The fact that the church does not fully understand that the lives of believers in CHRIST should be dictated by LOVE, is abit disturbing. And on top of that, some churches teach the heretical doctrine that 'GOD The HOLY SPIRIT' is an unnecessary add on (however the WORD of GOD teaches us that the workings of GOD The HOLY SPIRIT is an integral part in the lives of believers)! So if you attend church services at a building that claims that GOD The HOLY SPIRIT is not needed for that church to 'advance' the gospel, you need to disassociate yourself from that mess. That institution is laying the groundwork for a trap to spring on you, because the Bible says exactly the opposite of what that church is teaching! The Bible is not going to lie to you [but certain cino's will]!

John 16:8-9

> 8 And He, when He (GOD The HOLY SPIRIT) comes, will convict the world about [the guilt of] sin [and the need for a Savior], and about righteousness, and about judgment: 9 about sin [and the true nature of (sin) it], because they do not believe in Me [and My message]

Another fairly large 'faux pas' is that they (the cino church system) do not teach how to pray correctly. The corrupt system already had two strikes against it, but to the list of being insubordinate to the KING and trying to negate what the KING said now we find out that the cino churches purposefully do not teach people how that they can communicate with The KING?

In **Mathew 6** JESUS is talking about how GOD looks inside of our hearts and when a person is able to give a grandiose prayer that is repeated on the lips only to impress other people, we are told that GOD is not moved by those types of prayers (aka: king James prayers). JESUS talks about how when people give to charity, the giver should not act like a peacock and hope to be seen by another person (showboating). Time and again, JESUS keeps emphasizing how our communications/prayers to GOD should not be just words, but a persons words need to come from a compassionate heart.

1 Samuel 16:7.

> ....The LORD does not look at the things people look at. People look at the outward appearance, but the LORD looks at the heart.

And then the church teaches that JESUS taught people that to talk to GOD they needs to memorize a formula of words? A person would think that the church would realize that real prayers to GOD come from the lives of people. That is what is meant by **1 Thessalonians 5:17** "Pray without ceasing". Do you think that GOD will be impressed if you don't come up for air? Maby people should have an all night prayer meeting, surely GOD will receive our communications if we do not go to sleep at night! Ha...real prayer is about bowing your heart to the KING (a person does that by showing Love to other people). A person is in constant communication with GOD when

LOVE oozes out of that persons life Prayer is not an on/off switch. Fans have an on/off switch, beating hearts do not. A living person can not choose for there heart to only beat on certain days. A beating heart is a beacon that indicates a living person, just like the greatest prayer that a true believer in CHRIST prayers is done by living.

Sometimes history mixes with legend, but the story is told that Robert the Bruce died in 1329 (at the age of 54). The story says that when Robert the Bruce died, his heart was removed and embalmed. The heart was placed in a container and carried into battle by James Douglas. In an ill-fated battle Douglas was surrounded. Douglas garbed the heart and commanded his solider to "fight for the heart of your king" as Douglas flung the heart into the midst of the enemy.

I know that cino's look like Kingdomites (on the outside). But the heart beat of cino's sound like this "thump, thump, thump, thump", but the hearts of Kingdomites sound like this "LOVE, LOVE, LOVE, LOVE". It might not be a difference that many people are able to physically observe.

Some people might know the story of Cain and Able. Cain put up with his brother as long as he was Able (Ha...see what I did there!) But GOD says something interesting.

Genesis 4:10

> The LORD said, "What have you done? The voice of your brother's [innocent] blood is crying out to Me from the ground [for justice].

Some people might say that the verse is nonsensical...well, no its not. (I encourage people to read about the scientific findings) we do not have a ton of knowledge about this sound, but different molecules of 'DNA' has a unique frequency. While most humans might not be able to distinguish blood based solely on sound resonance, GOD can. I also want to point out:

2 Corinthians 5:17

> *Therefore if anyone is in Christ, he is a new creature; the old things passed away; behold, new things have come.*

In the verse above the word 'new' means new (it is not referring to 'new to me' like something that you purchased at a second hand shop.) Also the phrase 'old things have passed away' that means that some things got old and the died.

Another grievance that many churches are guilty of is the fact the majority of churches act like they have a 'new and improved' version of the bible. Consider this, hands down JESUS CHRIST was the greatest preacher...ever! Traditional 'pastors' would have people believe that although church growth is measured by the number of warm bodies that are present, the real numbers game is about how that church can reach as many people as possible with the gospel (although I would argue that many churches don't even understand what the gospel message is). But right now we are going to explore what many churches view as a reliable model of 'church growth'. The greatest preacher focused on 12 men, and more specifically 3 men (Peter, James, John). I realize that JESUS preached to many people, but JESUS poured HIS life into 12 men. So JESUS taught us that to effectively revolutionize the world, we need to go deep. I am not talking about a surface level howdy-doody message that is preached once a week. I am talking about depth, the kind of depth that comes from spending time with each other. I do not think that most churches even know, who among them has certain food allergies, but we should be concerned about the welfare of the people that are around us. I think that many people act like Cain and they ask 'am I my brothers keeper' (Genesis 4:9). This message goes out to all of the self centered C.I.N.O's...YES you are your brothers keeper! I am going to say something, and listen to me. One of the most effective 'churches' that many people engage in is 'family time'.

It is more than a little unfortunate that the church system is laboring to build the kingdom, meanwhile the blueprints that they are using are the instructions from a game of playing cards. Actually, its kind of funny...I say that because the church should probably get some sort of trophy for being such a colossal failure. Think about the irony of the situation...the same institution that has claimed to be the leading representative for the kingdom, come to find out is not even trying to follow the battle plan of the KING....that is pathetic humorous! Its almost as if some church do not have any business being the 'caller' in the game of -Simon Says-.

Now that we have examined one of the more comical attributes that the church system posses (and by attributes I mean...pretty much the whole thing), I would like for us to direct our attention to a more serious piece of business. JESUS is my KING! The KING does not make suggestions or recommendations. The KING issues orders that must be followed (It just so happens that this is the reason why many people do not want to be followers of the Messiah. I think that the majority of folks would be happy to be part of a kingdom that is all about love, many people want JESUS to be their SAVIOR...they just do not want to admit that JESUS is the CHRIST/KING.)

If someone claims to be a member of the KING's Kingdom and does not follow what the KING has said...that person is a traitor! In my opinion the C.I.N.O churches are more despicable than the heathen, because at least the heathen will openly admit that they want nothing to do with CHRIST, however the C.I.N.O's try to invent an imaginary world where they pretend to stand in the protection of the KING but in practice they do not want to follow the orders of the KING. **THIS IS WHAT THE WORD OF THE LORD SAYS**:

Revelation 3:15-16

> *15 I know your deeds, that you are neither cold nor hot. I wish you were either one or the other! 16 So, because you are lukewarm—neither hot nor cold—I am about to spit you out of my mouth.*

At times it good to remind myself about what JESUS said concerning the cino's in **Matthew 13:24-30**. I am aware that much of the church system refuses to teach the WORD of GOD, but it is not complicated. Many people that lived in Bible times were farmers and they were familiar with what a 'tare' is, but today a lot of people are not farmers. A 'tare' is just fake wheat, at first glance the wheatfield might look like it is full of good seed/good wheat. But upon closer examination a person will notice that what the field contains is some wheat and some weeds that look like wheat. To which the KING replies "Let the two grow together...for now".

Many people that have been indoctrinated by the church system and they think that the death, burial, and resurrection of JESUS is the entire point of the gospel. It is true that the Blood of JESUS is necessary for salvation. We know that JESUS knew that HE was going to be the sacrifice that would atone for the sins of HIS followers. However JESUS makes it clear that 'some sort of' power struggle existed, and JESUS came for the purpose of proving that HE is Boss. On one side of the battle is 'Truth' and on the other side is 'principalities and powers' **Colossians 2:15**. JESUS came to be the peoples champion that is on the side of Truth. Once JESUS had proved that HE is the KING (HE is the 100% undisputed victor),JESUS is even in charge of the grave (The principalities and powers felt certain that they were in control of death, but JESUS proved thoes guys wrong!) Remember in **Matthew 6:24**, JESUS talked about not being able to serve both GOD and be in love with the world, well JESUS came to prove that HE was the better of the two 'masters', but then JESUS hit them again and said 'do not think that I AM powerless after life is finished'! Assuming that JESUS came just to be a sacrifice for people's sins is like thinking that people visit amusement parks because they want to stand in line.

John 18:37

> So Pilate said to Him, "Then You are a King?" Jesus an-
> swered, "You say [correctly] that I am a King. This is why
> **I was born, and for this I have come into the world**, to
> testify to the truth. Everyone who is of the truth [who is
> a friend of the truth and belongs to the truth] hears and
> listens carefully to My voice."

JESUS did die for the remission of sins, but at the same time GOD bundled the sacrifice that JESUS made. Not only was a substitution made, but also JESUS mighty triumphed over the principalities and powers. Before JESUS came to earth HE already knew that HE was going to shed HIS Blood for our sins, but JESUS's earthly mission was to testify to the truth or proclaim The Kingdom of GOD (the kingdomites are drawn to the WORDs of our KING). Its like the institutionalized church have spent massive amounts of time and energy pointing to a tree, but actually its a forest!

One of the major pieces of evidence that show the church system does not even proclaim the same message that JESUS preached is that the the way that the system defines 'salvation'. If JESUS CHRIST was only interested in the 'after life' then HE would have sacrificed HIS life sooner. The way that the typical 'church' teaches, after conversion there is no purpose in living life. Maby people should exercise caution when being water baptized by the church system because they might just decide to hold you under a little while longer. Do you know the main theme of sermons that are found in the gospels...it goes like this "Repent"! What does the word repent mean? The word means 'get off the path that you are on', or remove yourself from the side that you are on and get on the side of Truth **John 18:37**. The main theme of the scriptures is that there are two waring kingdoms. You can only belong to one of the kingdoms, but every person that is sucking air is a member of one of the two kingdoms.

Matthew 6:24-25

> 24 "No one can serve two masters. For either he will hate the one and love the other, or else he will hold to the one and despise the other. You cannot serve God and money. 25 *"Therefore, I say to you, take no thought about your life, what you will eat, or what you will drink, nor about your body, what you will put on.* <Why should we not be overly obsessed with material things...because that is not the Kingdom that we are in!> *Is not life more than food and the body than clothing?*

Salvation is like signing up to join the army. Many church systems teach that the greatest contribution to 'Christianity' that most people give is just putting on the uniform!

Genesis 1:28

> *God blessed them and said to them, "Be fruitful and multiply, and replenish the earth and subdue it. Rule over the fish of the sea and over the birds of the air and over every living thing that moves on the earth."*

When a person goes fishing, the fish generally do not jump into the boat by themselves (although Asian carp do), and when a person goes hunting most of the animals will not 'freeze' when a warning shot is fired into the air. So why do christians think that they are being world changers just because they are wearing the 'christian uniform'?

Remember that I said that JESUS was pointing out the fact that 'some sort of' power struggle existed **Ephesians 6:12**. On one side of the battle is 'Truth' and on the other side is 'principalities and powers'. Some churches teach that scripture and people only hear the first part "We do not wrestle against flesh and blood" and they think 'that good news because I excel at sitting around doing nothing'. People like that love to put on the uniform and go to the pep rallies, but when it comes time to actually 'effect change' those people have adopted a 'laissez-faire ' form of leadership. JESUS came to be the peoples champion that is on the side of Truth. I must have missed the sermon where JESUS explains that its a good thing that HE arrived because HE was going to sacrifice HIS own life for us so that so called christians could put on the uniform and sit on the bench. Scripture makes it clear that salvation has always been about faith **Genesis 15:6**. Even the 'salvation' message that the church system proclaims is a flawed message. However the church system is doing a really good job at producing bleacher bumps.

It is obvious that GOD rescuing the children of Israel from Egyptian bondage is a shadow of GOD rescuing HIS children from the clutches of this word (that is salvation). If the salvation that JESUS came to earth to point to was compared to a 1,000 piece jigsaw puzzle, then the institutionalized church has spent a lot of time trying to build a table that will hold the box that the jigsaw puzzle came in. I am not saying that salvation is not important, I am just pointing out that many churches are codling 'christians' and I am pretty sure that the KING does not like that **Matthew 25:14-30**.

Before I become to upset because of what the C.I.N.O's have done, let me remind us all that true believers in CHRIST are in positions and they are laboring diligently. The WORDS of the KING are:

Matthew 13:27-30

> *27 So the servants of the householder came and said unto him, Sir, didst not thou sow good seed in thy field? from whence then hath it **tares**? 28 He said unto them, An enemy hath done this. The servants said unto him, Wilt thou then that we go and gather them up? 29 But he said, Nay; lest while ye gather up the **tares**, ye root up also the wheat with them. 30 Let both grow together until the harvest: and in the time of harvest I will say to the reapers, Gather ye together first the **tares**, and bind them in bundles to burn them: but gather the wheat into my barn.*

Before people hear the words of some snake oil salesman that tries to claim that the above passage is referring to when the Christians will be separated from the vile heathen, allow me first to appeal to reason, a tare is not an ordinary weed. A tare is a tricky weed that appears to look like a head of wheat. Even JESUS said that 'C.I.N.O's were going to be growing right next to the good wheat. I would do well to remind myself that although C.I.N.O's can be annoying and give incorrect information to people, it is all in the plan of GOD. GOD is patient and long suffering and when HE spots injustice being committed sometimes HE just sits back. We ask GOD why HE did not strike the injustice, the answer is that GOD's cup of wrath is not yet full (I need to ask for forgiveness because if GOD was as patient with me as I am with other people, then GOD probably would have already turned me into a grease spot.)

The next grievance that I have against the industrialized church is their actions mock the work of CHRIST. I think that I have been to funeral services that are more lively than most communion services. First most church services are led by some num-nut minister that tries to act like they are trying to get nominated for an Oscar by announcing 'they murdered JESUS'! No one murdered JESUS! Talk about poking JESUS in the eye, can those people not read what JESUS said...

John 10:18

> **No one takes it** *(my life) from me, but **I lay it down** of my own accord. **I have authority to lay it down and authority to take it up again.** This command I received from my Father.*

It is almost as if such people only know how to 'cherry-pick' certain Biblical passages. Listening to many C.I.N.O preachers are like listening to the arguments of progressive-democrats. A person tries to be polite and listen to them but at the end of the day their most persuasive arguments are really just efforts to manipulate a persons emotions.

Hebrews 12:1^b-2

> *...let us run with endurance and active persistence the race that is set before us,* 2 [looking away from all that will distract us](for example pay no mind to momentary discomfort) *focusing our eyes on Jesus, who is the Author and Perfecter of faith* [the first incentive for our belief and the One who brings our faith to maturity], *who for the joy* [of accomplishing the goal] *set before Him endured the cross, disregarding the shame, and sat down at the right hand of the throne of God* [revealing His deity, His authority, and the completion of His work].

Many preachers claim to have some level of Biblical knowledge, but they are Biblical novices. Besides not correctly dividing the WORD of GOD **2 Timothy 2:15**, the other problem is that they have parked. Life is like a hill, and people are like cars that have no breaks. It is impossible to not either be going up the hill or down the hill, but C.I.N.O's reason that they can maintain membership in the Kingdom of GOD while they 'drift' through life...but they are wrong **2 Peter 2:4-10**.

According to **Matthew 26:29** JESUS had gathered together with HIS disciples in an event that is known as the last supper. The way that CHRIST pours HIS LOVE on the true Body of Christ is the example that has been given to godly males, as it pertains to marriage **Ephesians 5:25**. Just like CHRIST LOVED the (true) Church, husbands are supposed to Love there wives. Show me a sane wife that would be remorseful because her husband preformed an act of valor? I will point at such insanity when I mention that the institutionalized church teaches people that communion should be a somber time. The husband of the true Church faced a shameful death on the cross, and HE could not stop thinking about spending eternity with HIS Bride (the joy set before HIM) **Hebrews 12:2**. JESUS who is the LOVER of our souls, just got done telling us that HE was going to wait and not participate in drinking from the vine until all of us are united in The Kingdom **Matthew 26:29**....what part of what was done screams cry fest?

To JESUS: I want to say that I think what you done was heroic and in my book the actions that YOU took deserves a medal! I consider it an honor to know that YOU refuse to taste the fruit of the vine until we can share the experience together.

Your friend:

Travis :)

I have been involved in my fair share of awkward situations and I am going to share a tip that I have picked up. Whenever an event takes place and you are not sure what the appropriate reaction should be...then try to mimic what the smartest guy in the room is doing. And GOD is clearly the smartest guy in the room, so lets look at how GOD reacted to JESUS sacrificing HIS life.

Isaiah 53:10

> Still, it's what GOD had in mind all along, to crush him with pain. The plan was that he (JESUS) give himself as an offering for sin so that he'd see life come from it—life, life, and more life. And GOD's plan will deeply prosper through him (JESUS).

Before mankind was even created, GOD already knew that mankind was going to make a bad decision and eat the forbidden fruit. GOD knew that HE could not stand being around even a trace of sin, and mankind can not 'clean themselves up'. So from the beginning GOD had a plan to clean up (redeem) mankind, the plan was for GOD HIMSELF to send HIS SON JESUS on a rescue mission. The Bible explains to us that GOD took pleasure in seeing HIS SON become the fall guy. GOD knew that without JESUS (who is GOD in the flesh), all of humanity was destined for hell. I am able to understand the emotional roller coaster of what it feels like to mentally want to balance the facts that; 1) JESUS CHRIST was totally innocent of any wrongdoing, and 2) knowing that the only thing that stands between hell and myself is the guilt free SON of GOD that shed HIS blood for me. It is almost easy for me to not be sure how I feel about the situation. However GOD is the smartest guy that is in the room, and I imagine that Heaven was running victory laps during JESUS's crucifixion. So, raise your glass high and rejoice that JESUS's BLOOD was shed and HIS Body was broken. If GOD had not broken HIMSELF...then I would have had to face the full wrath of a Righteous GOD!

Hebrews 12:2 explains to us that JESUS is our ultimate role model, and when hell told JESUS 'we are going to snuff your life out' JESUS said "you guys have no idea how much terror I am about to unleash".

John 10:18

> *No one can take my life from me*. *I sacrifice it voluntarily.*
> *For I have the authority to lay it down when I want to*
> *and also to take it up again. For this is what my Father*
> *has commanded."*

Stop repeating what the church system cries out by saying 'we killed the SON of GOD' because that is not true, in fact I think that it is like slapping JESUS in the face. Stop trying to downplay the glorious actions of our heroic KING! At no point did mankind have the power to snuff the life out of The SON of GOD. JESUS gladly laid down HIS life and then HE gladly picked HIS life back up!

I am able to understand what Gandhi was saying. Many people believe that they are a 'christian because they have walked into a church building, but that idea is like a person thinking that they are a car mechanic just because they own a wrench.

"I like your Christ, I do not like your Christians. Your Christians are so unlike your Christ."

— Mahatma Gandhi

Do not be fooled by imitations, only one true KING exists. Follow the Words of the KING and not some snake oil salesman that claims to belong to a 'church'. I have good news to share with people, our KING has overcame the world! By coming to earth, JESUS established a trail. The name of the trail is The Kingdom of GOD, and I have Good News! JESUS has made it possible for people to follow the trail that HE established.

Wichcraft in the Church

Witchcraft is defined as: the exercise or invocation of supernatural powers to control people or events.

In this section I am going to present the case that many foundational beliefs that many church institutions teach is simply what I refer to as 'christian wichcraft'. I will use scripture to point out that many 'churches' have replaced the GOD of Abraham, Isach, and Jacob while they have inserted a 'god' of there own invention.

If a person has 10 gallons of ice cream in container 'A', and has 1 gallon of crap in container 'B' After the two containers get mixed together then the resulting product is 11 gallons of crap! I do not care if you produce a document that has 100 Holy Bible verses the moment that you add one sentence of your common 'opinion', then you have produced a document that is riddled with errors.

Ezekiel 44:23

> They (the church system) *are to teach my people the <u>difference between the holy and the common</u> and show them how to distinguish between the unclean and the clean.*

(Much of the modern church system can be described as the 'blind leading the blind'.) Much of the church system says that they operate in 'supernatural powers'. I am not trying to claim that the modern day church has 0% 'supernatural powers. However I am clearly pointing out that much of the church system is accessing the supernatural realm using 'the common'.

Some people might assume witches need to have wort's on there noses, and put all sorts of items into a cauldron and boil the liquid together, and that might be true in certain situations. But if we use the definition that is listed above, then rubbing a lamp and being hopeful that a genie will come out of the lamp is a form of witchcraft (and 'a wish' is exactly how much of the church defines Faith). So is planing your days based on your horoscope. Anytime that a person preforms an action for the purpose of recruiting a undefined mystical force to act on their behalf, then that is witchcraft. (Here is to sending positive vibrations your way!) Perhaps someone might ask 'when a person prays to GOD for help is that witchcraft?'. Well the answer is not that straight forward.

Take for example little Johnny. Johnny has a big test at school tomorrow, however Johnny chooses to not study and instead spends the evening playing video games. When he arrives at school the teacher hands out the test, but before Johnny begins he bows his head and asks 'god' to bless his ignorance and fill his head with knowledge. Johnny has been taught that 'god' is simply the giant Santa Clause in the sky. No wonder why so many church goers like to celebrate christmas. The church system has taught many people that christmas is that special day when 'the santa clause god' extends his benevolence. The santa clause god spends all year 'blessing' church goers, but at christmas time his benevolence is extended to all of the good boy and girls.

Romans 12:9-13

> *9 Let love be without hypocrisy. Hate what is evil. Cleave*
> *to what is good. 10 Be devoted to one another with*
> *brotherly love; prefer one another in honor, 11 <u>do not</u>*

be lazy in diligence, be fervent in spirit, serve the Lord,
12 rejoice in hope, be patient in suffering, persevere in
prayer, 13 contribute to the needs of the saints, practice
hospitality.

I believe that 'witchcraft' depends on a persons heart, but in the above example Johnny put 0% effort into trying to succeed. It seems to me that Johnny is practicing a form of witchcraft. Setting aside the fact that Johnny may not realize that his lifestyle is in direct disobedience of the order that the KING gave, Johnny is reaching into the spiritual world and asking 'something' to guide him. What Johnny is doing is preforming the same shenanigans as thoes that are involved in the 'new age religion' are involved in. I realize that Johnny has been taught that his incantations are words called 'praying', but the Bible teaches us that we are to try to not be mentally sloppy. A person should live in constant communication with GOD **1 Thessalonians 5:17**, and I am very aware that some people are just poor test takers. But the way that Johnny is trying to pimp GOD, he is treating 'prayer' like a magic lamp. Such a person is not walking prayer.

Colossians 3:23-24

23 Whatever you do, <u>work at it with all your heart</u>, as
working for the Lord, not for human masters, 24 since
you know that you will receive an inheritance from the
Lord as a reward. It is the Lord Christ you are serving.

It is my belief that much of modern day christianity invests a lot of time serving a counterfeit 'god'.

Many churchgoers are taught to be in love with the idea of 'faith', but there is a disconnect between hearing and doing (Such behavior is not good **James 1:22**). Unfortunately, bad behavior tends to spread.

The C.I.N.O preachers have figured out how to multiply. They teach a bleacher bump 'christianity'. The main thing that bleacher bump christians do is they sit on the bleachers!

In **Deuteronomy 11** we can read a portion of the Bible that is known as the 'table of blessings and curses'. Lets take verses 13-17 and use them as an example. In verse 14-15 GOD says that HE will preform a positive action, but the positive action will only be preformed if people will follow the commands of the LORD. In verse 16 GOD tells the people that they should be sober minded because there is imitations of GOD, but if people started to follow the imitations and did not follow the commands of the LORD then that would make GOD angry. As a result, the blessing that GOD gave would turn into a curse.

Deuteronomy 11:13-17

> 13 "It shall come about, <u>if you listen obediently to my commandments</u> which I am commanding you today, to love the LORD your God and to serve Him with all your heart and all your soul, 14 that He will give the rain for your land in its season, the early and late rain, that you may gather in your grain and your new wine and your oil. 15 He will give grass in your fields for your cattle, and you will eat and be satisfied. 16 <u>Beware that your hearts are not deceived</u>, and that you do not turn away and serve other gods and worship them. 17 Or the anger of the LORD will be kindled against you, and He will shut up the heavens so that there will be no rain and the ground will not yield its fruit; and <u>you will perish quickly from the good land</u> which the LORD is giving you.

'Christian' Witchcraft is accepting an imitation. A lot of preachers/

ministers teach that 'Lets all imagine the best possible outcome and we will call that a God thing'. But GOD has given a prescribed path to approach HIM. I know of an event that took place where a Hindu, a Muslim, and a Christian were all asked to pronounce a blessing over the event. I was told that the Hindu and the Muslim both gave inspiring and moving speeches that began like this 'Oh god we know that your are in everything yet you are im-material', but when the Christian prayed the prayer began like this "**To the ONE whose NAME is above every other name, To the ONE who's NAME is the only NAME by which man can be saved"**. GOD is not a God that is among many other gods. GOD has a specific set of characteristics. But some churches act like approaching GOD is like playing with a "set of Lego's". Serving GOD is not like eating from a smorgasbord, you do not get to pick and choose what nice qualities that you think that GOD should have. Most church buildings that I have been in do not even attempt to preach the full council of GOD's WORD, instead you will be served a nice platter of 'the Lego god'.

I have observed that the majority of preachers have a 'circuit of scriptures'. The preacher might preach from the bible (actually, they might preach from part of the bible) and they paint a picture of what they think that 'God' looks like. Thoes preachers take pride in the fact that they are able to include a bible reference at the end of their half baked sermon. Its like building something and only following ever-other instruction in the blueprints, and then claiming ignorance about why you are experiencing crappy results. I once knew a 'preacher' whom did not include GOD The HOLY SPIRIT in his approved list of scriptures. I asked the man to let me hear his explanation of why The Bible says that receiving the infilling of GOD The HOLY SPIRIT is a natural progression that believers should follow **Acts 19:2**. I only heard words, but the words led me to believe that the man was pretty good at playing the game 'Twister'.

Acts 19:2

"Did you receive the Holy Spirit when you believed?" he asked them. "No," they replied, "we haven't even heard that there is a Holy Spirit."

The Bible explains attributes of GOD that none of us are able to fully understand, even if we had 500 lifetimes. But the difference is that some 'churches' do not want a bigger picture of 'god'. The motto of those people is 'if it does not fit, get a bigger hammer'. Some churches believe that they might not have a clear picture of who GOD is, but they think that they have mapped out the silhouette of God. Some people 'read the bible' because they want to confirm that the existence of the god that they have created

Call it what you will, but many churches are engaged in idolatry. Many preachers are teaching their congregants how to achieve success through 'christian wichcraft.' There is only one correct avenue for humans to engage the spiritual realm, and that avenue is laid out in the Bible. When I use the phrase 'laid out in the Bible', I mean the entire Bible. GOD does not change personalities.

Hebrews 13:8

Jesus Christ is the same yesterday, and today, and forever.

Certain people like to take words out of context, and then thoes people like to claim that they have a 'special' understanding of the nature of GOD.

So yoga is supposed to help calm a persons mind, but its wichcraft because an illegal avenue is being used. The same applies for psychics, mediums, fortunetellers, and tarot card readers. Wichcraft can involve rhythmic drum beats and human sacrifice, but at the heart...

wichcraft is just trying to send a message into the spiritual realm by means of an illegal method. Everybody that is alive is a spiritual being that is having a human experience (if the person dies then there human experience is finished). Some people try to make it sound fancy by giving it the name 'spirit guides' but if you are inviting another spirit to enter into your mind that is not good. Only one path exists for human beings to gain admittance into the spiritual arena, and the map for humans to find that path is told to us in the Bible.

Leviticus 10:1-2

> *Now Nadab and Abihu, the sons of Aaron, each took his censer and put fire in it, and put incense on it, and offered strange fire before the L*ORD, *which He*(GOD) *did not command them to do. 2 Then a fire came out from the L*ORD *and devoured them, and they died before the* L*ORD.*

Nadab and Abihu were two men that had been chosen by GOD to serve as priests. The two men were preforming there duties in the correct manner. But then The Glory of The LORD descended and at that point the two men apparently tried to add an exclamation mark to the end of what GOD was doing. The problem was that GOD did not want an exclamation mark...instead GOD wanted a period. GOD did not appreciate the 'extra gift' that was offered to HIM, instead GOD wanted people to just listen and follow the instructions that were given. But Nadab and Abihu were not careful to follow the commands of the LORD, they were not careful to distinguish between the Holy things and the common things **Ezekiel 44:23**. The extra gift that was not a 'Holy thing' is know as strange fire.

The big takeaway from the story is that GOD has a prescribed plan, and many church leaders teach that GOD does not concern

HIMSELF with the details. But the truth is that if GOD said 'make a hard right hand turn' then the order is to take a hard right hand turn. Now if you hear some slick eared preacher say 'I believe that God has allowed some wiggle room' and the order can be interpreted as 'take a gentle left or travel in a left hand position' and that person understands what GOD said, then that person is walking in apostasy.

Out of context preachers:

Hermeneutics is the study of how to properly interpret the Bible. Institutionalized churches do not understand personal boundaries, fortunately not every word that is recorded in the Bible is personally applicable to me'. To illustrate this concept a friend of mine showed me a picture of one of those 'inspirational biblical cards'. The picture contained the caption: "its less motivational when you know who said it". The actual card recorded the words that are found in **Mathew 4:9**. I can imagine that some unsuspecting person thinks that just because the Bible records the words "All this I will give you," he said, "if you will bow down and worship me." that it is a wholesome phrase to use, however the phrase is not 'inspirational' because satan said the phrase during the temptation of CHRIST.

I realize that some people that are in the church system try hard to logically approach the WORD of GOD, however there is a good number of voices coming from the church system that are not logical. Sometimes going to a 'church' and listening to a sermon is like going to Las Vegas and spinning the roulette wheel. Some ministers are so weak minded they make 'magic 8 balls' look intelligent. That is one of the reasons why I call those people 'C.I.N.Os' (christian in name only). I believe that JESUS addressed the cino's (pharisees) in Matthew.

Matthew 23:15

> Woe to you, [self-righteous] *scribes and Pharisees, hypo-*
> *crites, because you travel over sea and land to make a*
> *single proselyte* (convert to Judaism), *and when he be-*
> *comes a convert, you make him twice as much a son of*
> *hell as you are.*

Many ignorant people exist in the world, and many of the ignorant people blindly trust the cracker jack box that gave thoes clowns
ministerial licenses. As a result many people that have anything to do
with the church system, the 'biblical knowledge' that thoes people
have built upon a shoddy foundation.

Matthew 7:24-27

> *24 "Everyone then who hears* (James 1:22) *these words*
> *of mine and does them will be like a wise man who built*
> *his house on the rock* (anchored in the bed rock). *25 And*
> *the rain fell, and the floods came, and the winds blew*
> *and beat on that house, but it did not fall, because it had*
> *been founded on the rock. 26 And everyone who hears*
> *these words of mine and does not do them will be like a*
> *foolish man who built his house on the sand* (see foun-
> dation of The Leaning Tower of Pisa). *27 And the rain*
> *fell, and the floods came, and the winds blew and beat*
> *against that house, and it fell, and great was the fall of it."*

It is clear to see that GOD's WORD does not change **Malachi 3:6**.
What does change is how humans deal with things. GOD's WORD
is more solid than the price of gold, and the thoughts of mankind are
like paper money. People might think that the price of gold (GOD's
WORD) goes up and down, but what actually is happening is that the

value of paper money (the thoughts of mankind) is falling like a lead balloon!

In the 1950's a person that was especially jolly was described as being 'gay', by the 1990's mankind had changed the meaning of what a gay person was. So it would be incorrect for a person (that had a 1990's mindset) to read a letter that was written in the 1950's and point out all the 'gay' people. That is what some cino preachers do! They have little to no idea of any historical reference, they often reference a book in there sermons. The reference is usually cited quickly because like roaches and rats, cino preachers also prefer to deal underhandedly. The non-historical book that has completely no value but is still cited in many sermons is the book of '2 opinions'.

Many years ago I learned about 'absolute zero' (−273.15°C or −459.67°F). Absolute zero is defined as a complete absence of heat and motion. At one time science was having a difficult time at completely removing all of the heat from an object, so I asked the question why an ice cube could not lower the temperature even more. The problem with my question was that I did not understand that an ice cube (which freezes at 0°C or 32°F) would add a lot of heat to the equation. C.I.N.O preachers do not understand the purity of GOD's WORD. Like absolute zero, GOD's WORD is totally pure. If a 'good rule' is added to GOD's WORD then a lot of heat would be added to the equation. Not only are cino preachers passing along incorrect information about The KING and HIS Kingdom, but those churches are beginning to promote an entirely different gospel.

Tithing

I do not like the idea of thinking that we should put GOD on a 10% allowance. I do not like the compartmentalized view that says '_____ is GOD's share of the money the money, and _____ is my share of the money. **Psalms 24:1** explains that GOD is not interested in sharing in our 'wealth'. Society reflects that many churches teach this compartmentalized view of service to GOD. The incorrect teachings of many church organizations can be seen when **1 Thessaloians 5:17** is talked about. In that verse we are taught to *"Pray without ceasing."* According to the way that some preachers teach, the verse is difficult to do and some might question if JESUS spent all of HIS time in prayer. However, prayer is not a natural event. In the natural I only have 100% of my time, so if I sleep for 30% of the day then I am only able to devote 70% of my day to 'prayer'. So the command to *"Pray without ceasing"* is impossible to do as long as I remain in the natural. Since GOD is the Ruler of the Kingdom that is not natural (the Kingdom of GOD is supernatural), so I can be in prayer even when I am sleeping. Prayer is a condition of the heart. I will say it again, I have my doubts that certain churches even understand the concept of salvation.

A preacher that says that GOD wants to receive a 10% allotment of a persons finances, that preacher struggles with two concepts. First the preacher does not understand what it means for GOD to be KING (the KING owns it all), and the second issue that is not being understood is how the supernatural Kingdom operates. GOD does not want subjects of HIS Kingdom to be 10% committed, GOD does not even want a 90% commitment. GOD sees a persons heart! Even if you were able to give 100% of your paycheck, GOD would not be impressed if your heart was not in the right place **Mark 12:41-44**.

The Kingdom of GOD is not even in the same 'dimension' as the earth. However the actions that are preformed on the earthly dimension echo into The Kingdom of GOD. That is what is meant by:

Romans 8:3-4

> 3 *For what the law* (the law is another way of saying 'the old testament's code of conduct') *could not do, in that it*

was weak through the flesh (the law could only regulate the flesh)*, God did by sending His own Son in the likeness of sinful flesh, and concerning sin, He condemned sin in the flesh, 4 in order that the righteous requirement of the law might be fulfilled in us, who walk not according to the flesh but according to the Spirit.*

JESUS became the model for humanity to follow. I am more of a visual learner, and you can write the most detailed document explaining how to do something, and then when you see someone preform the action it becomes much more clear. Think about how complicated things could get when a person is trying to understand the difference between putting food into a 'microwave box' vs putting the food into the 'refrigerator box'. How about trying to explain a color to someone without out being able to point to or use the name of the color. Both examples might kind of be like explaining to someone what a mirror looks like.

The entirety of the 'old testament code of conduct' was written and all of those words had two points. #1 Love GOD, and #2 Love mankind. However the most well written rule book was unable to explain the concept of LOVE (why because LOVE is foundational!) Remember how JESUS said that the wise man builds his house upon the Rock **Matthew 7:24-27** (JESUS was not just teaching about construction). JESUS is the Rock or foundation, and there is nothing in the world that is able to explain LOVE. LOVE is the absolute foundation, there is no other foundation that is more perfect (or absolute) than LOVE. LOVE is the Rock bottom!

I like to think that I am a nice guy, but the niceness that I have did not originate with me. The niceness that I try to show towards other people is actually me copying GOD! GOD is the original source of LOVE and if I had never seen a picture of what GOD looked like, then

I would think that it is perfectly acceptable to deal treacherously with people. Of course when GOD sent HIS SON into the world it was like a giant projector in the sky, but even during the Old Testament GOD was showing people what LOVE looks like.

Jonah 3:10

> *When God saw what they did and how they* (The people from Nineveh) *turned from their evil ways, he* (GOD) *relented and did not bring on them the destruction he had threatened.*

When GOD would preform acts of kindness and mercy it would teach people how to treat each other **Luke 11:30**. (Also notice that GOD changed HIS mind. GOD had in mind that HE was going to demolish the Ninevites, and GOD told one of HIS prophets to deli-ever the message. Then humanity acted in such a way that made GOD change HIS mind...I am tired of the arrogant actions of pimple faced cino's treat the prophetic gifting like its a set of tarot cards. Some of the people do not even have an understanding of the nature of GOD, so they should probably sit down and shut up!)

I think that it would be easiest for me to begin unraveling the concept of tithing by starting the story before GOD delivered the Israelites out of Egypt. There was around 2.4 million former slaves that GOD liberated from Egypt, and the way that GOD organized those people was by 'tribes' (like extended family groups). Basicly 430 years before the Israelites left Egypt, all of the people were members of one big family. GOD basicly organized the Israelites into tribes that were named after each family member. Remember that GOD was using the Israelites to serve as a model of how HIS Kingdom is set up.

In the Kingdom model, GOD choose the family member that was named Levi to serve as the 'priestly tribe'. There were 12 tribes, but only members of the tribe of Levi were allowed to serve as the priests. Not only was the tribe of Levi to be the 'intermediary's between GOD and mankind, but also all of the people that belonged to the tribe of Levi were not to have a side hustle. So GOD did not design things to operate in such a way that someone was a priest/farmer a Levite was not even allowed to be a priest/landowner. 100% of the Levites income was to come from priestly duties. The Levites were not to serve in the army, nor were the Levites to share in the spoils of war. When GOD allowed the Israelites to possess the promised land the Levites were not given land to farm or hunt. GOD designed the Kingdom model so that Levites received 100% of their livelihood by serving as a intermediary between GOD and mankind.

At that time, there was not a 'governmental capital' and a 'religious capital'. Instead there was only one capital because GOD was the government. While GOD was explaining HIS Kingdom, the Israelites did not even have another form of government. In a way GOD made members of the tribe of Levi sort of like governors. In those days Israel did not have an I.R.S. (or a 'non federal' federal reserve bank). So GOD instituted a type of taxation that was set at 10% (a flat tax).

The system worked well for about the first 300 years, and then along came a politician named jeroboam (politicians have a way of messing things up). In a previous section I talked about the actions of what jeroboam did but in this section what jeroboam did makes about as much sense as 'fractional reserve banking', which the 'non federal' federal reserve bank forced down people's throats.

The concept of paying 10% of your income to support the government system/religious system, was crippled by jeroboam but it limped along for about 400 more years. Then a man by the name of jechonias was born and that man was so corrupt that GOD said that HE was going to erase the entire government that Israel had **Jeremiah 22:30**. Some time later GOD had the final book of the old testament wrote. The name of that book is **Malachi**, and the book of Malachi was written to address a corrupt priestly/governmental system. But tithing (or giving 10% of your income) was like a social program **Deuteronomy 26:12-13**. But to be clear, GOD abolished the corrupt governmental system that ancient Israel had **Jeremiah 22:30**, and then a book was written where GOD explained the problems that HE had with the corrupt system <entire book of **Malachi** >. One of the humorous parts (in my mind) is Malachi 2:3

Malachi 2:3; 5-8

> *3...I will spread dung on your faces, the dung of your festival offerings,... 5 "My covenant with Levi was* [one of] *life and peace, and I gave them to him as an object of reverence; so he* [and the priests] *feared Me and stood in reverent awe of My name. 6 True instruction was in Levi's mouth and injustice was not found on his lips. He walked with Me in peace and uprightness, and he turned many from wickedness. 7 For the lips of* <u>the priest should guard and preserve knowledge</u> [of My law], *and the people should seek instruction from his mouth; for he is the messenger of the L*ORD *of hosts. 8 But as for you* [priests], <u>*you have turned from the way and you have caused many to stumble by your instruction*</u> [in the law]. *You have violated the covenant of Levi," says the L*ORD *of hosts.*

In no way does GOD appreciate the job that the priests were doing. When GOD rates your job performance as 'worthy of having fecal matter smeared on your face', then the first thing that you want to do is stop 'trying' to do a good job. In **verse 10** GOD explains the level of betrayal of what has been done. Starting in verse 10 and continuing on until the close of the chapter (verse 17). GOD explains how what the preachers have done is like HIM finding out that HIS wife has been cheating on HIM. (GOD said that the example of how I am supposed to Love my wife can be seen in the LOVE that CHRIST shown towards the true 'Kingdomites'.)

In **Malachi 2:10-3:7** GOD gives a beautiful speech where HE explains that GOD had delighted in the early Levi, so GOD and Levi entered into a contract (GOD likens the contract to marriage vows). Then GOD explains that Levi (who was apart of Israel/Judah) started to not treat GOD like he did at first (GOD compares the actions of Judah like a young man who abandons the covenant that he made with his wife.)

In **Malachi 3:1-3** GOD explains that HE is going to put an end to the shenanigans that the priests had done. In **Malachi 3:2** GOD points out that the priests could not even follow a simple order and purify/launder what was being presented to GOD, so GOD was going to send JESUS. In chapter 1, GOD had explained that the priests had corrupted 'phase 1' of the Kingdom model that HE had laid out. So in verses 1-3 GOD explains how HE is going to move on to 'phase 2' of the Kingdom model, and a man named John the baptist was going to begin to shake/tear down phase 1 of the plan. Of course when JESUS CHRIST was sacrificed, at that moment GOD tore the veil in the temple and completely ended phase 1 **Matthew 27:51, Acts 17:24** (So why would I want to send money so that the temple can be rebuilt?)

Then in **Malachi 3:4** GOD takes a moment to talk about how once the corrupted phase 1 of the Kingdom model is cleared out of the way, GOD says the air will be fresh again. Once the cobwebs have been cleared from the attic and phase 1 is pushed aside then GOD will deal with the 'low life's' that pouted phase 1.

I am uncertain what the institutionalized church is trying to pull, but they somehow claim that GOD is encouraging mindless gifts to the priestly system...which GOD abolished. I guess the big take away is that the book of Malachi was written as a criticize to the priestly system so it is a not very thoughtful tactic to use any part of the book of **Malachi** to try to explain why giving tithes and offerings is Biblicaly mandated.

Malachi 3:8-10

> 8 *"Will a man rob God? Yet <u>you are robbing Me</u>! (Under the old covenant, only the priests offered things to GOD) But you say, 'How have we robbed You?' <u>In tithes and offerings</u>. 9 You are cursed with a curse, for you are robbing Me, the whole nation of you! 10 Bring the whole tithe into the storehouse, so that there may be food in My house...*

But I do think that a strong case can be made that GOD would like for someone to nail the doors of the church system shut, because they make GOD sick to HIS stomach.

Malachi 1:10

> *Oh that there were one among you who would <u>shut the doors</u>, that you might <u>not kindle fire on my altar</u> in vain! <u>I have no pleasure in you</u>, says the LORD of hosts, and <u>I will not accept an offering</u> from your hand.*

I think that I am limited in what I can do, but my best FRIEND seems to be asking for assistance. So I am going to give what aid that I am able to give! This message goes out to all of the true Kingdomites, the tithes and offerings that you are giving/paying is most likely supporting a money laundering scheme. The overwhelmingly majority of 'church leadership' has turned into a group of business executives (many of whom preform quite poorly). It is my belief that each persons 'money' is in need of a job, and if we incorrectly assume that the church system is gainful employment for our dollars...I imagine that GOD will deal with our actions appropriately **Matthew 25:14-30**.

I would like to talk about 'Guilt by Association'. GOD has a perfect track record. If GOD said that HE was going to throw a pie over HIS left shoulder, and the pie was going to be thrown with such force that it will hit you in the back of the head...well don't take HIS WORDs lightly! When GOD becomes agitated by the actions of a group of people and HE yells out things like "I will rebuke your decedents" and "I will smear poop on your face" **Malachi 2:2-4**...that's a group of 'friends' that you do not need to be hanging out with! What I am trying to point out is that when ever a person supports a fraudulent system then that person is no longer able to claim that they are an innocent bystander. They have moved themselves into the 'willing participant' category. Each person is giving a vote of confidence when they 'donate' their tithe/offerings.

But I guess I should not be to surprised by what the church system is doing because GOD already foretold that unscrupulous individuals would try to re-ignite the abominable sacrificial system that has been offered to The LORD **Malachi 1:4**.

Pre-tribulation rapture theory

A clear example of the behavior that many in the modern day church system practice is laid out I **Malachi 2:9**.

> ...I have caused you to be despised and humiliated before all the people, because you have not followed my

ways but have shown partiality (a special fondness, preference, or liking) *in matters of the law.*

What GOD is pointing out is the fact that there are over 31,000 verses in the Bible and most people that are involved in the church system have hand selected 50 (or so) verses and based their entire belief system on the verses that they have chosen to listen to.

The Pre-tribulation rapture theory makes perfect sense if a person only reads part of the bible. A person is even able to proclaim that the pre-tribulation rapture is a biblical teaching because it is in the bible. Many church followers approach the bible like the Center for Disease Control explains things...both institutions explain a story, never mind that its only partially true. The important thing is that the story contains truth. Its the example that I have said before **'If nine gallons of ice cream exists and you top off the container with a gallon of crap... then which end of the container do you want to begin eating?'**

Many preachers teach that it does not matter what a person believes in respect to when JESUS is coming back for the True Church. I have listened to many hucksters claim that 'JESUS must be returning before the anti-christ. That argument is know as a pre-trib. belief system or that JESUS will return to earth before (pre-) the tribulation (trib.). Believers in the pre-trib. theory, claim that 'the church' is not mentioned after **Revelation 3:22**. The rock solid logic of the pre-trib belief system holds up for the next nine chapters.

Revelation 13:7

> *It was granted to him* (the anti-christ system) *to wage war with the saints and to overcome them. And authority was given him over every tribe and tongue and nation*

It is almost cute how pre-tribers argument is that they can not imagine why a series of letters were sent to various churches, and then why suddenly 'the church' is no longer the center of attention. To be clear the pre-trib. rapture theory believes that all of the saints of GOD will have left earth and be totally out of the reach of the anti-christ...so the pre-trib rapture theory is not a Biblical concept!

That would be like someone claiming that because the bible records the words that were spoken in **Matthew 4:9** every believer is able to make a claim and take possession of said things.

Matthew 4:8-9

> *8 Again, the devil *took Him to a very high mountain and *showed Him all the kingdoms of the world and their glory; 9 and he said to Him, "All these things I will give You, if You fall down and worship me."*

When talking to people that have an attention span that's about as long as an inch worm its probably best to try and not introduce ideas that are built upon abstract concepts. I will say this, stop relying on the logic of individuals that are not even familiar with the text that they are teaching.

Cessationism

Cessationism is the view that the "miracle gifts" of tongues and healing have ceased after the end of the apostolic age. Most cessationists believe that, while God can and still does perform miracles today, the Holy Spirit no longer uses individuals to perform miraculous signs. Those Gelatin heads, think that the 70 years between the outpouring of GOD the HOLY SPIRIT up until the death of John the apostle was a totally unique time period [those guys would be good bridge salesmen]. Those theological Dodo birds must have been absent from school the day that **1 Peter 1:23-25** was discussed.

1 Peter 1:23-25

> *23 Being born again, not of corruptible seed, but of incorruptible, by the word of God, which liveth and abideth for ever. 24 For all flesh is as grass, and all the glory of man as the flower of grass. The grass withereth, and the flower thereof falleth away: 25 But <u>the word of the Lord endureth for ever</u>. And this is the word which by the gospel is preached unto you.*

After a certain amount of offenses a person stops being an ignorant buffoon and appears as a two headed snake. Certain people should excuse themselves from the gene pool, but those people are doing the crappie flop in the kiddy pool. They are confident in the ability of there arm floaters to keep their heads above water, meanwhile they are putting the 'P' in the word pool!.

For thousands of years it has been evident that without the intervention of GOD, then there would be no Kingdom of GOD. For that reason the disciples asked JESUS when HE was going to 'whip things into shape' **Acts 1:6.**. The disciples were thinking that the Kingdom of GOD was like a game of chess. In the game of chess the king is infinitely valuable, and the rules state that the entire game is won or lost based on what the king piece did, but GOD set HIS Kingdom up differently. The question that the disciples asked would have been appropriate in every other kingdom. But when the disciples asked KING JESUS when The KING was going to 'stand-up' and silence HIS opponents, JESUS responded by saying 'don't expect me to do all of the work'.

Some churches arrogantly proclaim that GOD THE HOLY SPIRIT

is no longer in the business of empowering Kingdomites. It makes a person wonder what a church denomination that believes in the load of crap called called cessationism is trying to do? I would suggest that perhaps they have not read **John 16:7-8**, but the sad truth is that I think many have read the passage and they choose to ignore what it says.

John 16:7-8

> *6 But because I have said these things to you, sorrow has filled your heart. 7 But I tell you the truth, it is to your advantage that I go away; for if I do not go away, the <u>Helper</u> (GOD THE HOLY SPIRIT) will not come to you; but if I go, I will send <u>Him</u> to you. 8 And <u>He</u>, when He comes, <u>will convict the world</u> concerning sin and righteousness and judgment*

I know that much of the Southern Baptist church denomination does not believe that they need GOD THE HOLY SPIRIT to convict the world of sin. Many in the Baptists church believes that it is their jobs to convict people. Things get really ridiculous whenever the Baptist church starts praying that the 'god' that they have chopped into pieces would send revival to their church. I am unsure what those people think will happen, but they almost seem sincere when they think GOD THE HOLY SPIRIT (whom they believe no longer operates) will take a break from HIS 'hiatus' to visit them to have tea and crumpets!

The incorrect doctrine of eternal security

Eternal security, also known as "once saved, always saved", is the belief that from the moment anyone becomes a Christian, that person is immune from hell. That incredibly ridiculous belief states that 'once a person experiences salvation' it is impossible for that person to 'forfeit' their salvation.

In **Matthew 25**, JESUS gives an illustration of how The Kingdom of GOD is organized. And we are told that the KINGDOM will not tolerate slackers. If you present to the KING exactly the same valuable asset then the KING will have you thrown into hell! So if the KING places an item of value in your care, and then you decide to not try to multiply the value of said item...then the KING can and will throw that lazy bum into hell!

Matthew 25:14-29

> *14 "For it* ("IT" refers to the Kingdom of GOD) *is just like a man* (The man is GOD who is The KING) *about to go on a journey, who called his own slaves* (The true Christians or Kingdomites) *and entrusted his posses-sions* (talents) *to them. 15 To one he gave five talents, to another, two, and to another, one, each accord-ing to his own ability; and he went on his journey. 16 Immediately the one who had received the five talents went and traded with them, and gained five more tal-ents. 17 In the same manner the one who had received the two talents gained two more. 18 But he who re-ceived the one talent went away, and dug a hole in the ground and hid his master's money. 19 "Now after a long time the master of those slaves came and settled accounts with them. 20 The one who had received the five talents came up and brought five more talents, saying, 'Master, you entrusted five talents to me. See, I have gained five more talents.' 21 His master said to him, 'Well done, good and faithful slave. You were faith-ful with a few things, I will put you in charge of many*

things; enter into the joy of your master.' 22 "Also the one who had received the two talents came up and said, 'Master, you entrusted two talents to me. See, I have gained two more talents.' 23 His master said to him, 'Well done, good and faithful slave. You were faithful with a few things, I will put you in charge of many things; enter into the joy of your master.' 24 "And the one also who had received the one talent came up and said, 'Master, I knew you to be a hard man, reaping where you did not sow and gathering where you scattered no seed. 25 And I was afraid, and went away and hid your talent in the ground. See, you have what is yours.' 26 "But his master answered and said to him, 'You wicked, lazy slave, you knew that I reap where I did not sow and gather where I scattered no seed. 27 Then you ought to have put my money in the bank, and on my arrival I would have received my money back with interest. 28 Therefore take away the talent from him, and give it to the one who has the ten talents.' 29 "For to everyone who has, more shall be given, and he will have an abundance; but from the one who does not have, even what he does have shall be taken away. 30 Throw out the worthless slave into the outer darkness; in that place there will be weeping and gnashing of teeth.

<see also> **Matthew 22:1-8, Matthew 24:45-51, Matthew 8:12, Matthew 13:36-43, Luke 13:25-26.** Today many 'churches' are led by people who are experts when it comes to dealing with sand, it just so happens that many of the 'sand experts' do not realize that sand is small rocks. Like JESUS said in **Matthew 23**.

How the above leads to witchcraft.

The Bible gives clear indication that certain beliefs are not of GOD. Snake oil salesmen exist (the ones that call themselves preachers) that teach that you can approach the 'god' of their bible any way that you see fit, but GOD does not want a person to approach HIM in a common way. Instead GOD requires a person that is sanctified.

Sanctify: to set apart to a sacred purpose or to religious use

Remember that everything that can be used to cut roast beef is not a steak knife, roast beef can be cut up with a lot of things that range from hair combs to screwdrivers. Your multi tool probably can slice roast beef, but do not insult my intelligence and say that you are carrying a steak knife! A steak knife is a utensil that has specifically designed to look nice enough to sit on the table in a dining environment also the knife needs to be able to cut through cooked meat. The purpose of the multi-tool is to be able to function in a multitude of environments. GOD does not want a drawer full of multi-tools.

Whenever someone is offering up service to GOD (Which should be all of the time!), the person should not serve GOD while wearing a pair of work gloves. If I describe to you a picture of a guy named Jeff that has a mustache, curly hair, and I tell you that every hair on the man is black. Then I show you the picture of the man and he is clean shaven and is bald. You will realize that the man that I was describing to you was not Jeff. What does it mean if two different groups of people are walking around and each group has a different idea of who Jeff is. The question becomes who is that bald man that was being described?

1 Peter 1:13-16

> *13 So get yourselves ready, prepare your minds to act, control yourselves, and look forward in hope as you*

focus on the grace that comes when Jesus the Anointed returns and is completely revealed to you. 14 Be like obedient children as you put aside the desires you used to pursue when you didn't know better. 15 Since the One who called you is holy, be holy in all you do. 16 For the Scripture says, "<u>You are to be holy, for I am holy</u>."

There are thousands of churches/religious institutions that are dedicated to worship, I am not debating that fact. What I am questioning is who they are worshiping. Those churches tell stories about the 'one' that they worship but the problem is that the god that they are worshiping is not the GOD that is described I the Bible. The god that those people serve does not mind if common elements are offered to it because they serve a common god! So be careful, just because the name on the sign says 'church' and inside they worship god...because there is a high probability that you are looking at a coven of witches.

Many churches are worshiping an imposter, whom they say will do _____ if a person sends tithe and offering money. To many people that are inside the church system they hand over money in exchange for protection (that's something that the mafia does), basicly many people are taught that the transfer of wealth is like the hand that rubs the lamp. Those misguided souls think that 'god' is a slot machine or he is a genie. A lot of the church system rescue teaches that god is like writing a blank check and people can just worship whatever idea they think god is. Some people are dreadfully afraid of experiencing any sort of hardship us, those people think that 'god' will allow them to escape earth before the tribulation starts...and there are many preachers that will contort scriptures to make a pre-tribulation rapture theory seem plausible. Some 'spiritual practitioners' are so spiritually anemic that they make a wet paper bag look like a bullet proof wall. It is not much of a mystery why those peoples have difficulty processing the fact that

GOD is still a miracle worker. Today there are scam artists that will claim to be preachers that are more than willing to teach droves of people that 'god' suddenly changed his mind about supernaturally healing people. Remember how the the Bible often says 'if – then' statements, for example 'if you do such and such then GOD will respond in this manner'. Well some preachers are such big boneheads that they have tried to change GOD's 'if – then' statements.

Exodus 15:26

> *"And said, If thou wilt diligently hearken to the voice of the LORD thy God, and wilt do that which is right in his sight, and wilt give ear to his commandments, and keep all his statutes, I will put none of these diseases upon thee, which I have brought upon the Egyptians: for I am the LORD that healeth thee."*

I kind of feel like making a shirt for people like that, but I don't think that they would want to wear it. So you be the judge, when people like that 'pray that their god' would send revival, what do you think that GOD feels like sending them! (I know...I know that some people will see the word judge and scream 'the preacher at church told us that people are not supposed to judge matters'. I have been trying to explain that a good majority of those charlatans only claim to have Bible knowledge **1 Corinthians 6:3**.)

Witchcraft is defined as: the exercise or invocation of supernatural powers to control people or events.

If anybody thinks something that I said is worth repeating then go ahead and repeat my words. An individual might want to use some of what I said in a speech, or someone might see the need to reprint my words...either way is fine by me.

Lightning Source UK Ltd.
Milton Keynes UK
UKHW020641240521
384271UK00011B/834